Atlas of Race, Ancestry, and Religion in 21st-Century Florida

Florida A&M University, Tallahassee
Florida Atlantic University, Boca Raton
Florida Gulf Coast University, Ft. Myers
Florida International University, Miami
Florida State University, Tallahassee
University of Central Florida, Orlando
University of Florida, Gainesville
University of North Florida, Jacksonville
University of South Florida, Tampa
University of West Florida, Pensacola

Atlas of Race, Ancestry, and Religion in 21st-Century Florida

Morton D. Winsberg

Urban Cartography by Jeff Ueland

University Press of Florida
Gainesville/Tallahassee/Tampa/Boca Raton
Pensacola/Orlando/Miami/Jacksonville/Ft. Myers

Copyright 2006 by Morton D. Winsberg
Printed in the United States of America on recycled, acid-free paper

11 10 09 08 07 06   6 5 4 3 2 1

A record of cataloging-in-publication data is available from the Library of Congress.
ISBN 0-8130-2929-5

The University Press of Florida is the scholarly publishing agency for the State
University System of Florida, comprising Florida A&M University, Florida Atlantic
University, Florida Gulf Coast University, Florida International University, Florida
State University, University of Central Florida, University of Florida, University of
North Florida, University of South Florida, and University of West Florida.

University Press of Florida
15 Northwest 15th Street
Gainesville, FL 32611-2079
http://www.upf.com

Contents

5. Racial and Ancestry Distributions within Florida's Large Urban Areas

Figures

Tables

Acknowledgments

I am indebted to members of the Florida Resources and Environmental Analysis Center at Florida State University, particularly Peter Krafft and Betsy Purdum for their technical and editorial advice. The staff of Florida State University's Division of Documents and Special Collections was extremely helpful. Special thanks must go to Judy Depew who patiently helped me obtain population data from the Internet. Faculty and staff of Florida State University's Department of Geography generously assisted me in resolving many of the technical problems that accompany the construction of an atlas. Shawn Lewers deserves particular recognition. Peter Vincent of England's Lancaster University provided invaluable critical advice, and the University of Miami's Ira Sheskin supplied some of the religious data. I am also grateful to David Graham of the University Press of Florida who established how to execute the maps in a graphics program and determined their color schemes. I am also grateful to my copyeditor, Nevil Parker, who greatly improved my manuscript.

Introduction

This atlas responds to Floridians' need to better understand the racial, ancestral, and religious complexity of their state's population. Divided into two sections, the atlas first identifies the Florida counties where various racial, ancestral, and religious groups are overrepresented. Here, "overrepresentation" means that, in 2000, a group's share in a county's population was at least 25 percent higher than the group's share in the state's population. Because Florida's population is highly concentrated in relatively few places (Fig. I.1), I chose to use maps that identify where groups are overrepresented, rather than dot distribution maps that show where groups are actually located. Expressed as dot distributions, each group's discrete population map would have been almost indistinguishable from that of the state's total population distribution. In the second section of the atlas, however, dot distribution maps *do* appear. Here, using census tract data, the maps show the distribution of selected racial and ancestry groups within the state's four major urban regions: Gold Coast (Miami-Dade, Broward, and Palm Beach counties); Tampa Bay (Hillsborough, Pinellas, Pasco, and Hernando counties); Orlando (Lake, Seminole, Orange, and Osceola counties); and Jacksonville (Nassau, Duval, Clay, and St. Johns counties).

Today Florida is among the most racially and ethnically complex states in the nation. This was not always true. Before 1950, Florida demographically resembled other southern states whose populations consisted mainly of whites (mostly of Anglo Saxon or Celtic origin) and blacks. Prior to that decade, most of the people who moved to Florida came from other parts of the South. During the 1950s, however, the rivulet of Florida newcomers from other parts of the country became a great river. Among those arriving were a growing number of non-Hispanic white retirees.

Since 1959, the number of Hispanics coming to Florida has risen dramatically. At first, most were exiles from Castro's revolution in Cuba. Over time, as economic conditions deteriorated elsewhere in Latin America and civil unrest intensified, many more from that region arrived, some from as far south as Argentina. While Latin Americans continue to be the principal source of foreign immigrants to the state, millions have arrived from elsewhere, especially from the non-Hispanic islands of the Caribbean. Today, an estimated three million people born outside the United States live in Florida, about 20 percent of its total population.

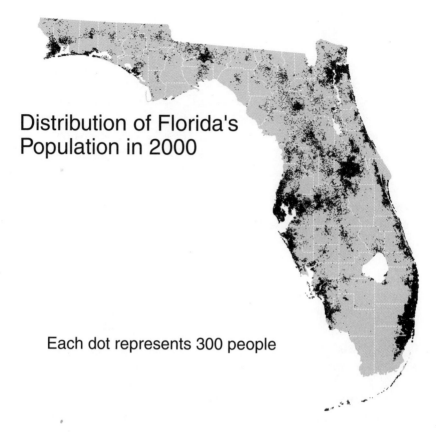

Fig. I.1. Dot distribution map of Florida, 2000. Map drawn by the Florida Resources and Environmental Analysis Center, Florida State University, Tallahassee, Fla.

Of the more than two million Florida residents who arrived in the United States after 1965, most have settled in its three southeastern counties: Miami-Dade, Broward, and Palm Beach. The image of Miami as a Latino city has become so indelibly imprinted in American minds that it isn't hard to understand why many of us, including Floridians, know little about the racial and ancestral diversity of other parts of the state. News media often draw the nation's attention to a Miami in crisis—to the city's race riots, for example, or to Haitians' protests over what they perceive as the greater opportunities enjoyed by immigrants from Cuba. We recall the Mariel boat lift tumult of 1980 and from 2000, the struggle of Miami's Cuban population to keep six-year-old Elián Gonzalez from being returned to his father in Cuba. Then, of course, there is the Miami defined by popular culture. On a positive note, Miami was put on the nation's musical map by the Cuban-born singer Gloria Estefan who, with her musician husband Emilio, gained national fame for the musical style produced by their Miami Sound Machine. During the 1980s, the popular TV police series *Miami Vice* did much to project an image of the city as both racially and ethnically complex *and* exceedingly violent. *CSI: Miami*, a more recent television series, perpetuates that theme. Hollywood has not ignored the city's colorful underside. Perhaps the best-known film about that milieu is *Scarface*. Filmed in 1983, it traces the rise and fall of a young Miami Cuban cocaine lord played by Al Pacino.

Miami-Dade County's population is the largest of any county in Florida. Even so, while it has more people from many ancestral and racial groups than

Fig. I.2. Florida counties. Map drawn by Florida Resources and Environmental Analysis Center, Florida State University, Tallahassee, Fla.

Fig. I.3. Cities and towns of Florida.

other counties throughout the state, the percentage of some of these groups in Miami-Dade's population is smaller than their percentage within the populations of other, much less populated counties. To appreciate the degree of racial and ancestral diversity found elsewhere in the state, this atlas, using data from the 2000 U.S. Census of population, identifies counties where the percentage of racial and ancestry groups in the population is substantially higher than their percentage in the total state population. In addition, using county data collected by the research unit of the Roman Catholic Glenmary Home Missioners, I include maps depicting those counties with exceptionally high percentages of adherents to Florida's largest religious denominations. Florida has become well known for attracting non-Hispanic white retirees from elsewhere in the nation. Although this group's ancestry is highly diverse, the atlas includes a map identifying the counties where these retirees are unusually well represented in the total population, and I discuss their changing distribution over time.

Most Floridians now live in the state's four largest metropolitan regions: the Gold Coast, Tampa–St. Petersburg, Orlando, and Jacksonville. For some of Florida's racial and ancestry groups, the combined share of the four exceeds 75 percent of their state's population. I have included dot distribution maps in the atlas to show where within these urban areas some of the principal racial and ancestry groups live. The atlas begins with a brief history of Florida's population and goes on to interpret the contemporary spatial distribution of the groups portrayed on the maps.

Data

This atlas has drawn data on race and ancestry from the United States decennial censuses of population, particularly that of 2000. The *United States Census 2000*, more than any previous national census, provides a greater variety of information regarding the nation's racial and ancestry groups. All U.S. residents were enumerated using a questionnaire called the "short form" that was usually delivered through the mail. The short form asked basic questions about a respondent's ethnic group (Hispanic or non-Hispanic), age, sex, race, and household relationships. Whether they were Hispanic or non-Hispanic, all respondents were asked whether they were (1) white, (2) black or African-American, (3) American Indian or Alaskan Native, (4) Asian, (5) Native Hawaiian or other Pacific Islander, or (6) some other race. In previous censuses, the enumerated could only choose one race, but in 2000 they were permitted to choose more than one, even all six if they wished. Fortunately for comparability with other censuses, relatively few people chose to identify with more than one race. For the entire nation, the share of those with multiple racial identities was 2.4 percent, the same as it was for Florida. For Miami-Dade County, the most racially complex county in the state, the share was 3.8 percent.

The U.S. Census continues to racially categorize the nation's population despite the fact that social scientists regard human race more as a "social construction" than a term with biological meaning. Scientists have shown that there is a greater regional difference in the genes of blacks living in different parts of sub-Saharan Africa than there is between black Africans and Europeans. The U.S. Census acknowledges the problem of using the biological definition of race by including Asians among the six racial categories. The term "Asian," according to the census, includes all people hailing from nations regarded as part of Southeast Asia, the Far East, and the Indian Subcontinent. Clearly these Asian regions contain many people who fit colloquially within several racial categories. The point is, then, that there are many more racial combinations than an atlas can reasonably represent. The number of "Native Hawaiians and Other Pacific Islanders" living in Florida is so small, for example, that maps showing their distribution throughout the state are not included here.

The "long form" of the 2000 census was sent to one out of every six U.S. residents. Among its many question categories was "ancestry," defined by the census as "a person's ethnic origin or descent, 'roots', heritage, or the place of birth of the person, the person's parents, or their ancestors before their arrival in the United States." To social scientists, this definition is too broad; they narrow it to a group that continues to share a cultural heritage other than that of the majority culture. Of Americans who responded to ancestry questions, most are descended from immigrants who arrived so long ago that they share few if any of the cultural characteristics their ancestors originally imported. This especially applies to people of European ancestry: today, immigration to the United States from Europe is, with few exceptions, much reduced from what it was during earlier periods. Rather than "ancestry," the term "ethnicity" (at least as used in the social sciences) better applies to the new U.S. immigrants, who arrive mainly from other continents. Even among this large group, ancestry identification by country is inaccurate, because many countries have a number of ethnic groups living within them. For example, the census identifies the ancestry group Asian Indian, but within India there are numerous ethnic groups such as Brahman, Dravidian, Bengali, Gujarati, and many more. Immigrants from South Africa may be black and Zulu or Bantu, white and Boer or of some other European group, or white and Hindu.

Even with these caveats, the ancestry maps in this atlas make an important contribution to our understanding of cultural diversity in Florida. I have used the terms "ethnic" and "ethnicity" sparingly throughout the atlas, as they might apply to only one of a number of groups within a nation or, conversely, to a group that lives in more than one country. The 2000 census permitted respondents to choose multiple ancestries, and the Census Bureau therefore supplied its 2000 report with tables for both single and multiple ancestries. Most respondents, however, chose only one, and data for the maps and tables in this atlas are drawn from the 2000 census' single ancestry table. Only ancestry groups with 5,000 or more members living in Florida in 2000 are identified here.

The U.S. Census Bureau levied its last census of religion in 1936. Fortunately, through its research center, the Roman Catholic Glenmary Home Missioners, a society of priests, brothers, and sisters, has been gathering county data on religious denominations since 1952. To date, the center has conducted five censuses: 1952, 1971, 1980, 1990, and 2000. With each successive census, the center has been able to add more denominations. The most recent 2000 census includes 149 denominations, although requests were sent to 285. Unfortunately, there were at least 14 denominations, some with an estimated 100,000 or more adherents, that did not respond. Among these, many were black denominations. In effect, then, except for the relatively small number of blacks who worship within primarily white denominations, blacks have not been represented in the center's 2000 census. Consequently, I remind my readers—and because this point is so important, I will remind them again—that religious affiliation data in the atlas mainly represent white populations, and not even all of them. For example, predominantly white denominations such as the Church of God in Christ and the Jehovah's Witnesses did not participate. Despite its deficiencies, however, the Glenmary censuses are the most-often consulted by those who wish to know the size and location of the nation's religious denominations. Census data are available down to the county level and represent a large share of the nation's congregations and denominations, including members, adherents, and attendees. "Members" comprise those who formally belong to a church; "adherents" include all individuals in a county identified as belonging to a denomination; and number of "attendees" is based on average weekly worship attendance. My study uses the data on adherents. Undoubtedly much of these data are estimates and, in many cases, probably rough ones.

A Brief History of the Population of Florida

Colonial Period

The exact year that Europeans made first contact with Florida's native population is unknown. Contact almost certainly occurred before 1513, when the famous Juan Ponce de León expedition arrived. Although school children learn that Ponce de León arrived in search of the Fountain of Youth, this expeditionary leader's reconnaissance actually sought valuable resources to enrich the Spanish monarchy and, of course, himself. In 1521, Ponce de León returned to Florida with a royal charter to establish a colony, but he was wounded during an assault by hostile Indians and died shortly thereafter in Cuba. Several expeditions to Florida soon followed Ponce's, the most famous being that of Hernando de Soto. There was also a failed Spanish attempt to establish a settlement at the site of modern-day Pensacola. St. Augustine, founded by the Spanish in 1565, became the first European settlement in what would become the United States that has been continuously occupied to the present day. The city's founding was largely a response to French efforts to establish a colony near the site of today's Jacksonville.

Indians had been living in Florida for at least 12,000 years before Europeans came into contact with them. Florida's native population at the time the Spanish arrived has been variously estimated as between 150,000 and 350,000. Most Indians lived on the land between today's St. Augustine and Pensacola. When the Spanish arrived, those in the north were cultivating corn, beans, squash and other crops, although they still gathered wild plants, hunted, and fished. The Indians who lived farther south depended far more heavily on hunting, fishing, and gathering. Diseases, inadvertently introduced by the Spanish and to which the Indians had no resistance, quickly reduced the population to a fraction of what it was at the time of first European contact, greatly impeding the Indians' ability to resist the invaders.

The Spanish found little of value in Florida and only established two towns, St. Augustine and Pensacola, which they fortified. The town sites were chosen to prevent French and British incursions, and neither attained a civilian population much larger than 3,000 during the entire Spanish period. During the seventeenth century, to provision St. Augustine, as well as to convert the Indians to Roman Catholicism, a string of Franciscan missions was established between St. Augustine and the Apalachicola River, and friars began to proselytize among the North Florida tribes. At the beginning of the eighteenth century, the Spanish missions were overrun by English, who, along with their Indian allies, came in search of slaves escaped from Carolina plantations. The encroachers returned north not only with escaped slaves, but with many mission Indians as well. Later in the eighteenth century, in an attempt to repopulate Florida with Indians, the Spanish induced members of more northerly tribes such as the Creeks, and others from areas in present-day Georgia, to settle in Florida. Collectively, they assumed the tribal name *Seminole*, a word derived from the Spanish *cimmarones*, meaning wild ones.

Between 1763 and 1783, through a treaty with Spain, the British occupied Florida and in exchange relinquished Havana, which they had earlier captured from the Spanish. Historians generally agree that during the brief British period economic development within the colony, particularly along the St. Johns River, was more rapid than during the entire Spanish occupation that preceded it. During the British period, most of the Spanish left Florida, some with their slaves and Indian retainers. The British government awarded large land grants to privileged individuals who were expected to develop plantations for growing export crops, such as indigo and cotton, and to collect naval stores, particularly turpentine. One especially large plantation was established on the east coast south of St. Augustine and named New Smyrna. Its owner drew workers from the Mediterranean island of Minorca as well as from Italy and Greece. The plantation was not a success; most of the workers fled to St. Augustine, there forming a community where many of their descendants continue to live today. Most plantations did not use labor imported from Europe, but relied on slaves from plantations in the British colonies farther north or brought directly from Africa. Blacks greatly outnumbered whites in Florida throughout the British period. While most were slaves, the colony was, by then, home to a growing population of free blacks. During the American Revolution, St. Augustine also sheltered a number of loyalists who had fled from British colonies farther north.

British rule ended a year after Britain's defeat in the American Revolution, and the colony was returned to Spain. Florida remained under the rule of that nation until 1821 when it was ceded to the United States. Spain—by then impoverished from fighting wars at home and in futile efforts to retain control of most of its colonies—found it difficult to control events in Florida. As a result, Florida's population became far more ethnically diverse than it had been during the first Spanish period. A number of British subjects chose to remain in Florida when the colony was returned to Spain in 1783, among them loyalists from former colonies that had become part of the United States. Many whites from southern states, particularly Georgia, also arrived. Several urban censuses were taken during this period. In 1820, Pensacola had a population of 713, not including the Spanish garrison. Approximately one-third of this number was black. Half of the town's population had been born in Pensacola, but there were a number of people from Spain and its colonies, as well as a few from other European nations and the United States. Five from Africa were listed. There were also a few souls from Louisiana, presumably French Creoles. A census of St. Augustine taken in 1815, when 1,383 inhabitants were reported, identified one-third of the population as black and counted among the white population individuals from the United States, Spain, and other European countries.

Antebellum Period

After 1821 when Florida became a United States territory, its population grew more rapidly. Agriculture, primarily the cultivation of cotton and tobacco, was initially the main impetus for growth. Production concentrated heavily around Tallahassee, chosen as the new territorial capital because it was midway between the territory's two towns, St. Augustine and Pensacola. The region also happened to have clay soils appropriate for cotton and tobacco cultivation. During this early period, most of the white settlers descended from people who had come from the British Isles to colonize England's southern colonies between Virginia and Georgia. Some of the more affluent settlers arrived with slaves and established plantations. The majority, however, became small-scale family farmers or cattlemen on the frontier, where they frequently had to face Indian attacks. In 1845, when Florida was granted statehood, towns were few and small. Among its population of approximately 70,000 people, the vast majority lived in the northern part of the state (table 1.1) and almost half were black. Most blacks were slaves, born elsewhere in the South. In 1840, only 3 percent were free—a share considerably smaller than that during the second Spanish period. In fact, following its accession to the United States, many free blacks left Florida for Cuba. Although cotton continued to be the state's major cash crop, tobacco, open-range cattle grazing, and citrus production provided some of the best economic opportunities for those who arrived with little capital.

Florida's population growth was unlike that of most other territories incorporated into the United States at approximately the same time. Whereas

Table 1.1. Percent of total population by region, 1830–2000

Region[a]	1830	1840	1850	1860	1870	1880	1890	1900	1910
North Florida	90	93	88	79	71	76	62	62	58
North Gulf Coast					2	2	3	3	3
Space Coast							3	3	3
Gold Coast					3	4	5	4	5
Sun Coast							1	1	2
Peninsular Interior							22	20	19
Tampa–St. Petersburg					2	2	4	7	10
Rest of State	10	7	12	21	22	16	0	0	0
Total	100	100	100	100	100	100	100	100	100
Florida's population as % of U.S.	*	*	*	*	*	1	1	1	1

Region	1920	1930	1940	1950	1960	1970	1980	1990	2000
North Florida	51	38	37	33	25	21	18	17	17
North Gulf Coast	2	1	1	1	1	2	3	4	4
Space Coast	4	5	5	5	6	8	8	9	8
Gold Coast	9	17	21	26	31	34	34	32	32
Sun Coast	3	4	4	4	5	6	7	8	9
Peninsular Interior	19	20	18	17	16	15	16	17	18
Tampa–St. Petersburg	12	15	14	15	16	15	14	13	12
Rest of State	0	0	0	0	0	0	0	0	0
Total	100	100	100	100	100	100	100	100	100
Florida's population as % of U.S.	1	1	1	2	3	3	4	5	6

Source: U.S. Census.
Note: All dated columns rounded to the closest percent. Columns may not sum to 100 percent due to rounding. Before 1890, some regions had too few constituent counties to make possible the identification of percentage change.
*Less than 1 percent.

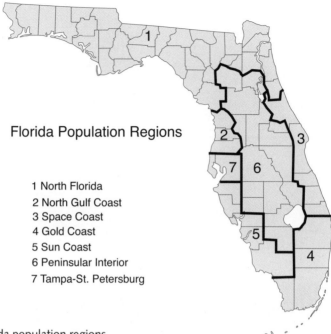

Florida Population Regions

1 North Florida
2 North Gulf Coast
3 Space Coast
4 Gold Coast
5 Sun Coast
6 Peninsular Interior
7 Tampa-St. Petersburg

Fig.1.1. Florida population regions.

most had enormous spurts of growth during the initial decades after entrance (followed by a substantial drop), Florida's initial rate of growth was not nearly so great. Between 1830 and 1840, Florida's growth rate was 54 percent, and between 1840 and 1850, it was 61 percent. For neighboring Alabama, the growth rate was 142 percent between 1820 and 1830, and 91 percent between 1830 and 1840. For Midwestern states, the rates of growth during the initial decades were much higher than even those of Alabama. Florida's decennial growth rates may have been initially smaller than these states, but in each decade up to the present they have continued to be markedly higher than those of the nation. The state's growth rate was highest in the 1960s, when the population grew by 79 percent.

Since 1920 the state has undergone an enormous redistribution of its population. This can be seen by an examination of table 1.1. Although some may take issue with the way the state here has been regionalized, the regions generally conform to the popular perception of how the state is geographically divided (fig. 1.1). Until the 1920s the state's greatest population concentration remained in the north. Jacksonville, Tallahassee, and Pensacola were North Florida's three most important cities. The port city of Jacksonville, at the mouth of the St. Johns River, was economically the region's most dynamic. The state's capital, Tallahassee, continued to be a market town for the fertile farming area nearby, while Pensacola's economic foundation rested heavily on its port, which shipped cotton and lumber produced in the city's hinterland. Despite North Florida's having the largest share of Florida's population, by the 1850s Key West had become the state's largest city, continuing in that position until the 1890s when it was exceeded in population by both Jacksonville and Pensacola.

First established as a naval station and later as a port for ships passing in and out of the Gulf of Mexico, Key West also attracted salvagers of ships that foundered on the Florida Keys. Quickly Key West's population became the most diverse of any city within the state. In 1870, almost half (44 percent) of the population of Monroe County—within which Key West was the only true town—consisted of foreign-born individuals. Most were from Cuba and the Bahamas. The city also had an unusually large number of Irish, though it is unclear whether they were Protestant or Catholic. Compared with the share of foreign-born within Florida's total population (3 percent), other coastal counties in the state had unusually high percentages of foreign-born residents. Franklin County (Apalachicola) reported 12 percent foreign-born; Escambia (Pensacola), 7 percent; St. Johns (St. Augustine), 5 percent; and Duval County (Jacksonville), 4 percent. Land-locked Leon County (Tallahassee) had less than 1 percent foreign-born. In most counties, people born out of state had come from one of the other southeastern states, most notably Georgia. The western Panhandle counties were the exception: the majority of those born elsewhere in the nation had arrived from Alabama.

Florida entered the Civil War on the side of the Confederacy, although a significant share of the state's population remained loyal to the Union. Despite being the Confederate state with the smallest population, Florida made a disproportionate contribution to the war effort, both in men and supplies, including salt and beef. Although it sustained less war damage than most of the other southern states, Florida emerged from the war equally impoverished, and the process of reconstruction was long and painful.

Civil War to the End of World War II

By 1880, Florida had recovered sufficiently from the war to begin to attract investment in, among other things, transportation. Although a skeletal network of railroads had been built before the Civil War, railroads were confined to the north. Roads were largely of sand and difficult to traverse. The only reliable form of transport on the peninsula was the steamboat, which provided transportation along Florida's coasts and on its navigable rivers, notably the St. Johns. By the 1880s, railroads began to penetrate south down the peninsula. The state facilitated their construction by offering land to railroad corporations at low prices. The corporations, believing land values along their lines would increase once the tracks were laid, were eager to buy. Furthermore, once sold, the land would generate freight and passengers for the trains. To encourage settlement on their lands, railroad companies advertised intensively throughout the United States, and even Europe, often exaggerating real estate potentials.

Many groves and vegetable farms were established during this period, and among their owners were people from northern states and particularly from the Midwest. Nonetheless, during the entire nineteenth century, the racial character of the state's population remained roughly the same: about 50 percent were identified in the censuses as white and 45 percent as black. Because the state's cheap black labor pool discouraged European immigration, most of the white population remained descended from colonial period immigrants to the southern states from the British Isles. There were, however, several attempts to organize colonies of foreigners within the state.

One of the earliest was an English colony established near Kissimmee in the 1880s that soon failed. In 1885, people from Scotland settled near Sarasota, but again the colony failed. A more successful colony was formed in St. Lucie County in 1893. The colonists were Danes from the Midwest. This colony survived, and at one time had over 1,000 inhabitants. Three years later, another colony of Danes, named Dania, was established in what is today Broward County. At about the same time, a failed effort was made to attract Swedes to Hallandale in northern Miami-Dade County. A Japanese colony, initially quite successful, was established in Palm Beach County in 1903. In 1911, a small community named Slavia, settled by Czechoslovakians, was founded northeast of Orlando on 1,200 acres. Later, in 1924, Czechoslovakians established another community near Tampa that they named Masaryktown. Despite these efforts, during the long period of enormous European migration to the United States (1880 to 1930), the share of Florida's foreign-born in its total population remained almost stationary at about 4 percent, far below that of the nation, which oscillated between 13 and 15 percent.

Cubans and Spaniards were two major exceptions to the low representation of foreign-born in the state's population. As a consequence of tariffs levied on

Table 1.2. Components of population change in Florida by decade: share of different groups in Florida's growth between 1880 and 2000

Population Groups (%)	1880–90	1890–1900	1900–10	1910–20	1920–30	1930–40
Non-Hispanic whites under 65	65	51	62	82	74	70
Non-Hispanic whites 65 and over	2	2	3	8	6	11
Blacks	33	47	35	10	20	19
Hispanics	ND	ND	ND	ND	ND	ND
Others	ND	ND	ND	ND	ND	ND
Total	100	100	100	100	100	100
Total population change	121,929	137,120	224,077	215,851	499,741	429,203

Population groups (%)	1940–50	1950–60	1960–70	1970–80	1980–90	1990–2000
Non-Hispanic whites under 65	79	73	47	48	45	33
Non-Hispanic whites 65 and over	11	14	21	21	18	10
Blacks	10	13	8	11	13	19
Hispanics	ND	ND	22	17	23	36[a]
Others	ND	ND	2	3	1	2
Total	100	100	100	100	100	100
Total population change	873,891	2,180,255	1,837,883	2,956,881	3,191,602	3,044,452

Note: ND=No data.

[a] Between 1990 and 2000, 22% of Hispanic growth was Puerto Rican, 19% Mexican, 14% Cuban, 5% Colombian, and 4% Venezuelan.

cigars (but not on tobacco leaves) imported into the United States and because of prolonged civil unrest in Cuba, during the 1860s cigar factories and their workers began to relocate to Key West. Most arrivals were Cuban-born, but others were Spanish immigrants who had originally gone to Cuba. Eventually the isolation of Key West from the rest of the nation, as well as labor disputes and several devastating fires, precipitated movement of cigar production to other parts of the state, particularly Tampa and, to a lesser extent, Jacksonville.

During the 1890s, after the pine forests of Michigan and Wisconsin had been largely cut over, some Swedish and Norwegian woodcutters from these states migrated to work in the yellow pine forests of the Panhandle. Other Scandinavians became involved in fishing along the Gulf Coast. During this decade an ethnic settlement that endures to the present began when people from the Levant—what is today Lebanon, Syria, Jordan, and Israel—arrived in the Tampa Bay area. Later, some of the Tampa group moved to Jacksonville and were joined by others who came from elsewhere in the United States or directly from the Levant. Greeks also came to Florida to dive for sponges in the Keys. When the Keys' sponge population collapsed because of disease, the Greek divers and their families moved to towns along the state's Gulf Coast, particularly the St. Petersburg area. Tarpon Springs is regionally famous for its Greek population, although few, if any, today remain engaged in the sponge industry.

The 1900 U.S. Census reports that 72 percent of the nation's 9,362 Cuban-born were living in Florida: 3,533 in Tampa and 3,059 in Key West. There were 4,011 Spaniards living in the United States, 27 percent in Florida. Most of the Spanish-born Floridians (963) lived in Tampa. Although Italians earlier had been brought to Kissimmee to work on a sugarcane farm, by 1890 many more had arrived in Tampa and were employed in its cigar factories. By 1900, Bahamians had spread northward along the Atlantic coast, up to Vero Beach. Most were employed in agriculture. In September 1928, hurricane winds over Lake Okeechobee created a surge of water that broke the dike protecting the agricultural area on the lake's south side. The flood that followed killed an estimated 1,800 people, many of them Bahamian field hands.

Data from the 1930 U.S. Census—taken at the close of the huge wave of immigration that began in the 1880s—quantifies the effects of this migration on Florida's population. Overall, the total share of foreign-born in Florida's population remained 4 percent, the same as it had been in 1870. The share was at that time 60 percent below the nation's share. There were, however, some important exceptions. The share of Spaniards in its total population was 7.6 times higher than the share of Spaniards in the total population of the nation. For Palestinians and Syrians, it was 17.4 times higher. For the combined total of Cubans and "other" West Indians, their share in Florida's total population was 6.8 times higher than their share in the nation's total population. In 1930, Miami-Dade County's (Miami) Little Havana had emerged, but the census enumerated only 483 Cuban residents within the entire county. That figure was greatly exceeded by their numbers living in Hillsborough (Tampa), Monroe (Key West), and Duval (Jacksonville) counties. Compared with the peninsula, West Florida—which had attracted many people from elsewhere in the South—continued to attract few foreigners.

Post–World War II Period

Florida's period of truly rapid population growth began after World War II (see table 1.1). Between 1940 and 1950, what previously had been one of the least populated southern states emerged as one exceeded in population only by four others. By 1960, Texas was the only southern state that had a larger population. In the 1980s Florida's population overtook those of Illinois, Ohio, and Pennsylvania, and in 1990 it became the fourth most populous state in the entire nation, exceeded only by California, New York, and Texas. Given the size of these states, it is doubtful that in the near future the population of Florida will be able to overtake any of them.

Initially, the two principal reasons for Florida's phenomenal post–World War II growth were an increase in the number of Americans who could afford to retire and live elsewhere and an increase in disposable income among younger people that permitted vacationing. We should not discount the widespread diffusion of air conditioning as an important factor in Florida's growth, as air conditioners have made the state's hot, humid summers far more endurable for residents and visitors. Other contributions to the state's growth include the federal government's policy to encourage home ownership through low interest loans and the state's well-organized effort at mosquito control.

Although Florida's attraction to retirees from northern states grew in the 1930s, the state became a major destination of retirees after World War II (see table 1.2). By then, many who reached retirement age could benefit from the Social Security pension plan that had been enacted by Congress in 1935. With Social Security and better private pension plans, more workers could entertain retiring from work and moving to other states. In 1930, the share of Florida's population 65 years of age and older was actually lower than this age cohort's share in the nation's population. By 1940, it was about the same, but by 1960 it was 60 percent higher (see table 1.2).

Florida's ability to attract non-Hispanic white retirees reached its peak in the 1970s and 1980s. During each of these decades the state added over one half million non-Hispanic white retirees to its population. By contrast, the 1990s was a decade of relatively slow growth among this age group. Partially this resulted from a decreased birth rate during the Great Depression and therefore fewer people reaching age 65, but this slowdown primarily was due to the fact that retirees now more frequently choose other southern states to retire in.

Immigration from abroad, particularly from elsewhere in the Americas, has become Florida's major growth component (see table 1.2). During the 1990s, the share of Hispanics overtook that of non-Hispanic whites under 65 years old. The black share, augmented by a large migration from Haiti, Jamaica, and other non-Hispanic Caribbean islands, also surpassed that of non-Hispanic retirees. The graying of Florida, so evident in earlier post–World War II decades, slowed markedly during the 1990s. After several decades during which the population was aging, Florida is now becoming more youthful. Although the share of people age 65 and older in its total population remains higher than that of the nation, by 2000 it was only 41 percent higher compared to 1970 when it was 60 percent higher. How this change in demographic configuration will affect future elections in Florida remains unknown.

For decades, the southern states were the principal source of migrants to Florida (table 1.3). After World War II, this pattern began to change. In the 1970s, the major source region became the northeastern states. During the 1990s, however, the arrival of foreign immigrants had become so large that their share in the in-migration to Florida almost equaled that of the northeastern states. The Midwestern states also have played an important role in populating Florida, but at least as many who left those states headed west as south. Arizona in particular became an important destination for retirees from the Midwest. By contrast, few people from the western states have chosen to resettle in Florida. Instead, in recent years, Florida has become incredibly attractive to people from Puerto Rico and abroad.

At first, most of the foreign-born people who came to live in Florida were Europeans, the majority having come to the United States long before they moved to the Sunshine State. By the 1960s, poverty and meager employment opportunities in the poorer nations had become so great that civil unrest began to spread. The first major stream of immigrants to Florida was from Cuba, following the successful social revolution led by Fidel Castro. At first, many

Table 1.3. Sources of Florida in-migrants (percentage of total in parentheses). Residence five years before census date

Years	Northeast States	Midwest States	Southern States	Western States	P.R. and Foreign	Total
1960	369,644 (30%)	308,492 (25%)	422,036 (34%)	57,765 (4%)	85,302 (7%)	1,243,239 (100%)
1970	390,961 (29%)	315,149 (23%)	363,852 (27%)	91,106 (7%)	181,084 (14%)	1,342,152 (100%)
1980	757,500 (37%)	472,891 (23%)	453,828 (22%)	117,143 (6%)	238,831 (12%)	2,040,193 (100%)
1990	805,018 (32%)	489,888 (19%)	641,896 (26%)	193,811 (8%)	389,868 (15%)	2,520,481 (100%)
2000	683,475 (27%)	398,223 (16%)	576,040 (23%)	203,034 (8%)	641,500 (26%)	2,502,272 (100%)

of these Cuban immigrants belonged to an economic elite escaping the newly installed Communist regime. During the 1950s, the number of Cuban-born to Florida increased by 21,909. Thereafter, the increase was much larger: in the 1960s it grew by 176,528; in the 1970s by 159,710; in the 1980s by 131,562; and in the 1990s by 144,632. Initially, the people comprising this immigration overwhelmingly came directly from Cuba. Now, many Cuban-born come from elsewhere in the United States, particularly from New Jersey and New York.

More foreign-born came to Florida during the 1990s than in any other decade. During that 10–year period, the increase was slightly more than one million people. The vast majority (80 percent) had been born elsewhere in the Americas. The nation that contributed the largest share was Cuba (14 percent), followed by Mexico (13 percent), Haiti (10 percent), Colombia (9 percent), and Jamaica (7 percent). Asian-born individuals, mainly from China and the Indian Subcontinent, contributed 11 percent of this growth, and European-born people provided an additional 7 percent. The remaining 2 percent came from Africa and Oceania. Although Puerto Ricans are not considered foreign-born, this group has recently become the state's fastest growing Hispanic population. Their numbers in Florida, which include those who identified themselves as Puerto Rican but were born in the United States, increased by 235,017 during the 1990s.

The large post–World War II migration to the state greatly altered the geographical distribution of its population. From the year Florida became a U.S. territory until 1900, the redistribution of the state's population was one of slow movement southward from its northern counties. Yet, even as late as 1920, the share of the state's population living in North Florida was 51 percent (see table 1.1). Thereafter, North Florida's share declined precipitously, and by 2000 it had fallen to 17 percent. Most of that redistribution has gone to the Gold Coast, where, between West Palm Beach and Miami, one of the nation's largest urban areas has formed. Florida's other coasts, however, have also increased their

Table 1.4 a–d. Regional share of four population groups, 1960, 1980, and 2000

Table a. Non-Hispanic whites less than 65 years old (%)

	1960	1980	2000
North Florida	23	21	21
North Gulf Coast	1	3	5
Space Coast	6	9	10
Gold Coast	32	26	21
Sun Coast	5	8	10
Peninsular Interior	16	18	20
Tampa–St. Petersburg	17	15	13
Total	100	100	100

Table b. Non-Hispanic whites aged 65 or older (%)

	1960	1980	2000
North Florida	13	9	12
North Gulf Coast	2	6	7
Space Coast	7	9	12
Gold Coast	34	35	23
Sun Coast	6	12	16
Peninsular Interior	14	12	17
Tampa–St. Petersburg	24	17	13
Total	100	100	100

Columns may not sum to 100 percent due to rounding.

Table c. Blacks (%)

	1960	1980	2000
North Florida	34	31	23
North Gulf Coast	1	1	*
Space Coast	6	7	5
Gold Coast	28	27	41
Sun Coast	3	4	4
Peninsular Interior	18	19	17
Tampa–St. Petersburg	10	11	10
Total	100	100	100

Table d. Hispanics (%)

	1960	1980	2000
North Florida	2	3	4
North Gulf Coast	*	1	1
Space Coast	*	2	3
Gold Coast	79	77	64
Sun Coast	*	3	5
Peninsular Interior	2	5	15
Tampa–St. Petersburg	17	9	8
Total	100	100	100

Note: * is less than 1/2 a percent.

shares of the state's population appreciably, as has the Peninsular Interior. The share of the state's population living in the Tampa–St. Petersburg region has fluctuated, but since 1960, it has gradually declined.

Interestingly, this redistribution has not been undertaken equally by all elements of the population. An examination of Florida's four largest groups (non-Hispanic whites younger than 65, non-Hispanic whites 65 and older, blacks, and Hispanics) reveals a considerable difference (see table 1.4). Between 1960 and 2000, the state's population grew by 11 million people, third behind California (18 million) and Texas (11.3 million). During this 40–year period, the share of non-Hispanic whites younger than 65 in Florida's total population fell dramatically on the Gold Coast and somewhat less in the Tampa–St. Petersburg region. It fell more slowly in North Florida. Growth was substantial in all other regions (table 1.4a). The redistribution of non-Hispanic whites 65 and older over this 40–year span resembled that of their younger age cohort. The shares of the Gold Coast and the Tampa–St. Petersburg regions fell sharply, while those of the Sun Coast, and to a lesser degree the North Gulf Coast and Space Coast regions, grew (table 1.4b). The share of blacks living in North Florida fell; that of the Gold Coast rose; and there was little change within the other regions (table 1:4c). The degree of the redistribution of the Hispanics between 1960 and 2000 might surprise those who believe that the Gold Coast holds the vast majority of this group (table 1.4d). While the share of Hispanics who live on the Gold Coast remains high, it has fallen significantly since 1960 when it was 79 percent. By 2000 it had fallen to two-thirds of the Hispanic population of the state. The group's share in the Tampa–St. Petersburg region also has fallen. The Peninsular Interior region has been the major beneficiary of the decline in shares of these two regions, but all the others have benefited as well.

2

County Population Concentrations

Introduction

Table 2.1 shows how Floridians identified themselves by race and ancestry in the 2000 census. As the U.S. Census uses it, the term race bears little relationship to its biological definition. In fact, most contemporary social and natural scientists reject racial definitions in relation to the population of the United States, because there has been so much intermarriage. Nonetheless, skin color and other physical characteristics remain powerful factors in shaping the nation's cultures and the Bureau of the Census continues to include the race question. In the 2000 census, the enumerated not only could choose their race, but they had the option of identifying themselves as of being of more than one. Only racial categories including 5,000 or more individuals living in Florida at the time of the 2000 census are identified in the atlas tables and maps.

As mentioned in the introduction, ancestry identification of the nation's population is also problematic. Although the 2000 census provides data on over 150 ancestry groups, they were derived, like race data, through questioning those enumerated. The ancestors of many Americans arrived so long ago that most people are an amalgamation of many ancestry groups. Those who chose to affiliate with one group often did so out of desire and not in reality. I reiterate here that the U.S. Census definition of "ancestry" cannot be used interchangeably with ethnicity. Despite its deficiencies, for want of any other data, ancestry has been used here in exploring the state's cultural diversity. Like racial groups, the ancestry groups represented in this atlas are limited to those that had 5,000 or more individuals living in Florida at the time of the 2000 census.

Table 2.1 shows the population of the state's racial and ancestry groups and their shares in Florida's total population compared to their shares in the nation's total population. Here we can see that the state has been most successful in attracting people from elsewhere in the Americas. Regarding ancestry groups, although Florida is the state with the fourth largest population in the nation, in 2000 it had the largest or second largest population in the nation of 31 ancestry groups. All but two of these groups (British and South African) were from the Americas.

Table 2.1. How Florida's population chooses to identify itself in 2000 (first race or ancestry)

Race	Population	Quotient
Total non-Hispanic	13,299,663	.95
Total Hispanic	**2,682,715**	**1.34**
Non-Hispanic white	10,456,458	.95
Hispanic white	**2,006,844**	**2.09**
Non-Hispanic black	2,244,701	1.17
Hispanic black	**67,404**	**1.77**
Non-Hispanic American Indian	54,428	.36
Hispanic American Indian	10,540	.48
Non-Hispanic Asian	320,803	.49
Hispanic Asian	12,210	.67
Non-Hispanic "other"	**128,927**	**1.28**
Hispanic "other"	568,927	.43
HISPANIC		
Argentinean	**22,881**	**4.00**
Brazilian	**32,636**	**3.52**
Chilean	**13,400**	**3.43**
Colombian	**138,768**	**5.20**
Costa Rican	**11,248**	**2.89**
Cuban	**833,120**	**11.83**
Dominican Republican	**70,968**	**1.64**
Ecuadorian	**23,939**	**1.62**
Guatemalan	**28,650**	**1.36**
Honduran	**41,229**	**3.34**
Mexican	363,925	.31
Nicaraguan	**79,559**	**7.89**
Panamanian	**15,117**	**2.91**
Other Central American	6,268	1.07
Peruvian	**44,026**	**3.32**
Puerto Rican	**482,027**	**2.50**
Salvadorian	20,701	.56
Venezuelan	**40,781**	**7.86**
Other South American Hispanics	**7,828**	**2.40**
OTHER WESTERN HEMISPHERE GROUPS		
Bahamian	**18,121**	**11.58**
British West Indian	**9,637**	**2.14**
Canadian	**47,596**	**1.74**
French Canadian	108,988	1.03
Guyanese	**10,885**	**1.27**
Haitian	**228,949**	**7.60**
Jamaican	**164,788**	**4.22**

continued

Table 2.1.—*Continued*

Race	Population	Quotient
Trinidadian and Tobagonian	**20,035**	**2.31**
United States or American	1,278,586	1.09
West Indian	**14,601**	**2.04**
West Indian (excluding Hispanics)	**469,014**	**4.77**
EUROPEAN		
Austrian	**35,078**	**1.42**
Belgian	10,120	.79
British	**64,078**	**1.30**
Czechoslovakian (including Slovak)	64,455	.73
Danish	28,541	.59
Dutch	122,308	.84
Eastern European	13,961	.99
English	1,040,033	1.10
European	85,183	.79
Finnish	18,328	.79
French (except Basque)	268,560	.97
German	1,291,500	.75
Greek	64,017	1.20
Hungarian	**66,758**	**1.30**
Irish	1,068,956	.98
Italian	843,872	1.15
Lithuanian	27,097	1.13
Norwegian	83,181	.45
Polish	304,809	.85
Portuguese	37,117	.71
Romanian	**20,545**	**1.35**
Russian	**156,284**	**1.43**
Scandinavian	10,190	.58
Scotch-Irish	190,660	1.02
Scotch	196,358	1.10
Spanish or Spaniard	40,288	1.22
Swedish	99,589	.72
Swiss	21,952	.72
Ukrainian	31,429	.83
Welsh	49,313	.98
Yugoslavian (also Croat, Macedonian, Serbian, Slovene)	13,527	.68
MIDDLE EASTERN AND NORTH AFRICAN		
Arab	65,544	1.13
Egyptian	6,178	.81
Iranian	8,755	.49
Israeli	**8,617**	**1.58**
Lebanese	24,152	1.22
Palestinian	**5,602**	**1.46**
Syrian	**7,649**	**1.27**
Turkish	**7,841**	**1.39**

Race	Population	Quotient
SUB-SAHARAN AFRICAN		
African	69,051	1.08
Nigerian	5,106	.56
Sub-Saharan African	84,696	.87
OTHER ASIAN		
Armenian	7,627	.40
Asian Indian	70,740	.74
Chinese (including Taiwanese)	46,368	.34
Filipino	54,310	.52
Japanese	10,897	.24
Korean	19,139	.31
Pakistani	5,299	.61
Thai	6,233	.97
Vietnamese (including Hmong)	33,308	.52
MISCELLANEOUS		
Non-Hispanic white, 65 and over	**2,326,014**	**1.47**

Note: Only groups of 5,000 or more are identified. Quotients represent the share of a group within the state's total population divided by the group's share in the nation's total population. Quotients of 1.25 or higher are highlighted.

The Races and Non-Hispanic Whites Over 65

Florida's racial composition has changed dramatically since World War II. Because the comparability of census race data between 1950 and 2000 is diminished by the fact that race is a social, not a biological construct in the United States and that among those enumerated, the definition has changed over time, this change cannot be measured with great precision. Nonetheless, the share of each race in Florida's total population at the beginning and end of this 50–year period invites comparison. In 1950, the population was 78 percent non-Hispanic white, 21 percent non-Hispanic black, while the remaining 1 percent included Asians, Hispanic whites, American Indians, and "others." By 2000, the non-Hispanic white share had fallen to 65 percent of the state's population, and the Hispanic white share had risen to 13 percent. In that year, the non-Hispanic black population had fallen to 14 percent, while the remaining 7 percent included mainly Asians, Hispanic blacks, and Hispanic "others." Most of the Hispanic "others" were Mexicans who identified themselves as of mixed race.

Non-Hispanic whites have always been the largest racial component of the state's population, although their share in the early nineteenth century was almost equaled by that of the blacks. The group's share in the state's total population began to decline during the 1960s following the growth of immigration from Latin America. Non-Hispanic whites continue to be overrepresented in the total population of a number of Florida's counties. Most of these counties have relatively small populations and are found along both the Gulf and Atlantic coasts. A large share of the non-Hispanic white residents of these counties are 65 years of age and older.

The non-Hispanic black share of the population of several Florida counties is markedly higher than their share in the state's population. This is particularly true of North Florida's Plantation Belt, so called because it was the state's principal cotton-growing region before the Civil War. From before the Civil War until after World War II, blacks dominated the populations of a number of Plantation Belt counties. By 2000, however, only Gadsden County continued to show black population dominance, although nearby counties have shares of blacks in their total populations almost as high as those of Gadsden County. Urban counties with large shares of blacks in 2000 were Duval County (Jacksonville), Broward County (Fort Lauderdale), and Miami-Dade County (Miami).

The distribution of non-Hispanic American Indians provides an opportunity to discuss how data on racial characteristics are derived. As previously mentioned, all recent censuses, including that of 2000, have been self-administered. Until recently, perhaps because of prevailing racial attitudes, few who filled out census forms chose to identify themselves as American Indian. Because for generations American Indians have intermarried with whites, many respondents probably came to believe that "white" was the most appropriate race to identify with. During the last 40 years, the nation has done much to eliminate racial and ethnic prejudice. Furthermore, in recent years, both in literature and film, Indian culture has become highly romanticized. An excellent example is the Kevin Costner film *Dances With Wolves*. Today many more Americans take pride in their American Indian ancestry and identify with it.

Throughout the twentieth century few Floridians identified themselves as Indian. In 1960, only 2,504 non-Hispanic Floridians identified themselves as belonging to that racial category. By 2000, that figure had risen to 54,428. Only a small part of this huge increase can be attributed to the two reasons for a change in population: natural causes and migration. It must follow then that in the 2000 census more non-Hispanics chose to identify themselves as American Indian than in previous ones. Counties where shares of non-Hispanic Indians are appreciably higher than the state average are mainly in northwest Florida, where most are descendants of the Indians who lived there during the colonial period. Another concentration is found on the west side of Lake Okeechobee, where several Seminole Indian reservations are situated.

Non-Hispanics who in the 2000 census chose either to identify their race as "other" or who affiliated with two or more races constituted only 2 percent of the state's non-Hispanic population. Among those included in the non-Hispanic "other" category were respondents who wrote in the blank box that they were multiracial, mixed, interracial, or any of several other terms that could not be matched with the form's five racial categories. In rank order, the three most popular race combination pairs were white–American Indian, white-Asian, and white-black.

Non-Hispanic white retirees constitute such a large share of the state's total population that it is appropriate to separate them from the total non-Hispanic white population and identify the counties in which they have concentrated. Retirees began to arrive in Florida in significant numbers even before World War II. Many chose to live in the Tampa–St. Petersburg region and on the Gold Coast, particularly in Miami-Dade County. The non-Hispanic white population age 65 and over first reached a share of a county's total population at least 50 percent higher than that of the nation's total in the counties of Pinellas, where St. Petersburg is located, and Highlands, then a rural county in the state's interior (fig. 2.1). Gradually, more counties reached that threshold and were included on the map. The majority that passed the threshold did so between 1960 and 1980, a period during which Florida became the leading destination of non-Hispanic white retirees in the nation. Since then—with the arrival of many younger people from elsewhere in the United States and abroad and with competition from other southeastern States for retirees—several counties have dropped below the threshold. The two most notable ones are Miami-Dade and Broward (Fort Lauderdale). Among the five counties that passed the threshold between 1980 and 2000 were two with large populations: Polk (Lakeland) and Brevard (Melbourne).

Since 1980 the Gold Coast's share of the state's non-Hispanic white retirees has been in decline. In 1980 it was 35 percent, but by 2000 it had fallen to 23 percent (see table 1.4b). In large part, this decline has been caused by the extraordinary growth of the region's younger population, particularly through migrations from the Caribbean. This influx of younger people has led to the same problems experienced within other large, densely populated urban areas—traffic congestion, high property values, and crime among them. The destruction wrought by Hurricane Andrew in 1992 to southern Miami-Dade County, a part of the county where many non-Hispanic white retirees lived, also hastened their departure. The share decline of Gold Coast retirees would

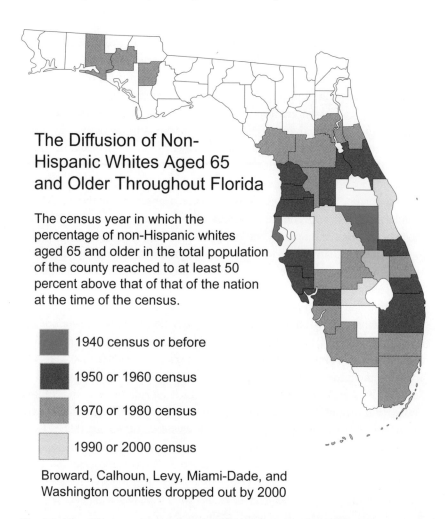

The Diffusion of Non-Hispanic Whites Aged 65 and Older Throughout Florida

The census year in which the percentage of non-Hispanic whites aged 65 and older in the total population of the county reached to at least 50 percent above that of that of the nation at the time of the census.

1940 census or before

1950 or 1960 census

1970 or 1980 census

1990 or 2000 census

Broward, Calhoun, Levy, Miami-Dade, and Washington counties dropped out by 2000

Fig. 2.1. The diffusion of non-Hispanic whites 65 years of age and older.

have been even greater had not the two other Gold Coast counties north of Miami-Dade County begun to attract them. Even so, by the 1990s, Broward County, which shares a border with Miami-Dade County, began to experience an absolute decline in the number of its non-Hispanic white elderly, a condition that Miami-Dade County began to experience during the previous decade. The group's population continues to grow in Palm Beach County. The Tampa Bay urban region's share of the state's retirees also has fallen, victim to some of the same problems experienced on the Gold Coast. In 1960, the region contained 24 percent of the state's non-Hispanic white retirees, but by 2000 it had fallen to 13 percent.

The regions that have been the major beneficiaries of the decline in shares of the state's two largest urban regions have been the Space and Sun coasts, as well as the northern part of the Peninsular Interior. Here, developers have been able to purchase large tracts of relatively cheap land (compared to land in counties with large cities) on which they have built communities designed specifically for retirees. Retirees who purchase homes in these communities not only benefit by the amenities that the developers provide, but by the less expensive housing made possible through economies earned from the large scale of development. Two counties, Alachua (Gainesville) and Leon (Tallahassee), both with major residential universities, have begun to attract retirees by emphasizing the cultural amenities their universities provide.

The distribution of Florida counties where the non-Hispanic white elderly are unusually well represented in their total population clearly reflects the group's attraction to the state's coasts. Except for Highlands County (Sebring), the only noncoastal counties where this group's share in the total county population exceeds that in the state's population are located in the upper portion of the Peninsular Interior: Lake (Leesburg), Marion (Ocala), and Sumter (Wildwood). All three experienced a spectacular growth in housing, most of it within planned urban developments designed for retirees. This was particularly true of Sumter County.

Since 2000, developers have been making a concerted effort to attract more white retirees to North Florida where there is an abundance of relatively inexpensive land, even near the coast. A number of large planned urban developments have been laid out recently along the Gulf Coast between Carrabelle and Pensacola. After decades during which the region's share of non-Hispanic white retirees declined, between 1980 and 2000 it rose three percentage points, to 12 percent.

The U.S. Census divided the Hispanic population by race in the same manner that it did the non-Hispanic. Most Hispanics who have settled in Florida (76 percent) have chosen to identify themselves as white. The second largest Hispanic group comprised the "other" category, where respondents usually described their race as mixed. Almost all of the remaining 3 percent chose their identity as black.

The Hispanic white share in the total population of only four counties is markedly higher than their share in the population of the state: Miami-Dade County (Miami), Osceola County (Kissimmee), Hardee (Wauchula), and Hendry (LaBelle). Hardee and Hendry counties are lightly populated and primarily agricultural, while Osceola County is a rapidly growing suburban county next to Orange County (Orlando). Miami-Dade County's exceptionally high share of Hispanic whites, compared to the state average, is due primarily to its huge Cuban population's being so deeply place oriented, a trait that will be explored in greater depth elsewhere, as will the enthusiasm among Puerto Ricans to settle in the Orlando area.

Mainly, it is in the state's interior counties that Hispanic "others" and those affiliated with two or more races constitute a far higher percentage of their total populations than the state average. Some counties have small and others large populations, but in all of them, agriculture is a major activity. Most agricultural workers in Florida today are of Mexican, Salvadorian, and Guatemalan origin. A comparison of maps for these three groups with that for Hispanic Others indicates the relationship of the former to the "other" racial category. Hispanic blacks are primarily urban, and Hispanic American Indians, who are small in number, are concentrated in many of the same counties as Hispanics who define themselves as "other" or of multiple races.

Latin American Ancestry

The use of "Spanish," "Hispanic," "Latino," and other terms to designate individuals from Latin America has encouraged the erroneous belief that in the United States they represent a cohesive ethnic group. Although they share many similarities, within Latin America there are considerable cultural differences both within and between nations. At times, hostilities have become so intense between nations that they have lead to warfare. Although these differences usually disappear once Hispanics reside in the United States, the significance of the national origin of Hispanics living in this country should be acknowledged.

Most Hispanics come to the United States in search of economic opportunities, either because a revolutionary government has deprived them of their livelihood or because their country's economic elite controls most of the wealth. In the case of Cuba, which had a successful social revolution in 1959, and Nicaragua, which had one in 1979, the governments that took power attempted to redress previous economic injustices through radical reform. This quickly led to mass emigration of the more affluent citizens of both nations. Currently, many of Venezuela's economic elite are leaving because of what they perceive as radical government solutions to problems faced by that nation's impoverished majority. Similarly, Colombia has experienced a long and bloody insurrection often described as a form of class warfare. Many among the Colombian economic elite have fled the country for the United States out

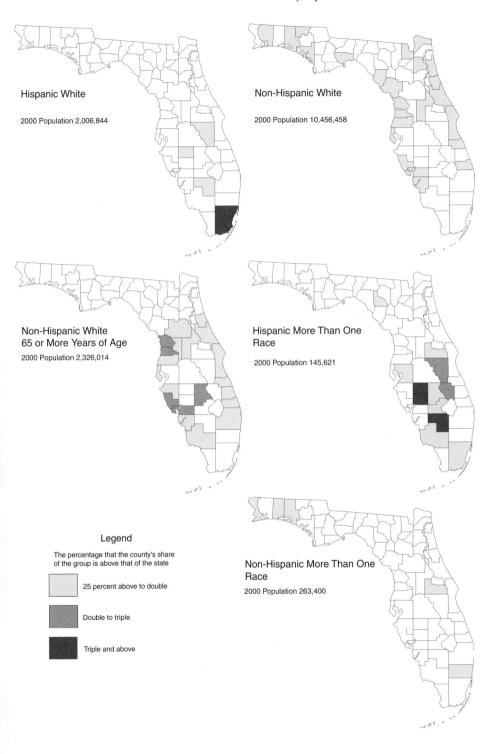

Hispanic White

2000 Population 2,006,844

Non-Hispanic White

2000 Population 10,456,458

Non-Hispanic White
65 or More Years of Age

2000 Population 2,326,014

Hispanic More Than One
Race

2000 Population 145,621

Legend

The percentage that the county's share
of the group is above that of the state

25 percent above to double

Double to triple

Triple and above

Non-Hispanic More Than One
Race

2000 Population 263,400

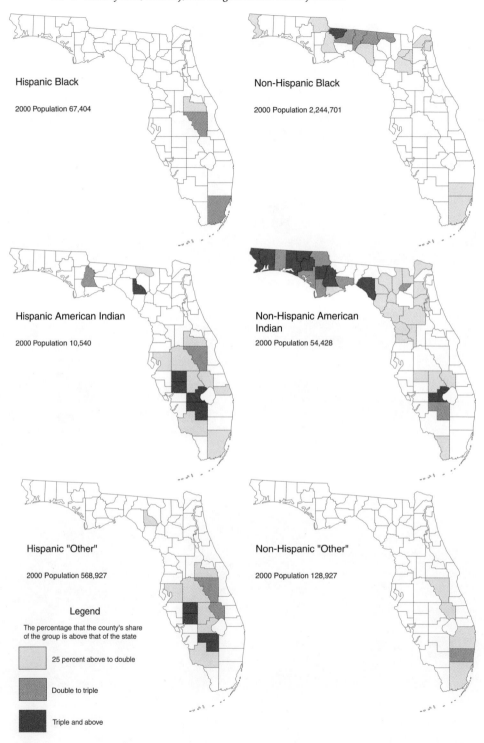

Hispanic Black

2000 Population 67,404

Non-Hispanic Black

2000 Population 2,244,701

Hispanic American Indian

2000 Population 10,540

Non-Hispanic American Indian

2000 Population 54,428

Hispanic "Other"

2000 Population 568,927

Non-Hispanic "Other"

2000 Population 128,927

Legend

The percentage that the county's share of the group is above that of the state

25 percent above to double

Double to triple

Triple and above

of fear of terrorism and kidnapping. The disparity in wealth between Mexico and the United States is arguably greater than that between any two neighboring countries in the world, so it is not difficult to understand why so many people from Mexico and other Latin American and Caribbean nations are so eager to come here to work.

The Gold Coast has exerted the strongest appeal of any Florida region on immigrants from Latin America and the Caribbean. Cubans, who formed the first large wave of immigrants to Florida, overwhelmingly chose to live in Miami-Dade County. Most of the first Cuban exiles found Miami a convenient place to settle, since they were convinced their exile would be brief. It was near Cuba and had a similar climate. More than 40 years later, Fidel Castro is still in power, and through immigration and natural increase the number of Cubans living on the Gold Coast has reached almost three-quarters of a million. The Hispanic environment created in Miami-Dade County by the Cubans has proven an inducement to many more Hispanics from elsewhere in the hemisphere to settle there. Today, Los Angeles County is the only other county in the nation where large populations of so many people from different parts of Latin America can be found.

Given that many Cubans arrived in South Florida by 1970 and have since raised families, we might expect their children, after leaving their parent's homes and establishing their own, to find work elsewhere in Florida or even farther away. Indicative of the strength of family ties among Cubans, their children who do leave Miami-Dade County often move to the neighboring Broward County. People who arrived in Miami from Honduras and Nicaragua also have shown little inclination to move elsewhere, nor have most of their children.

Within Florida, a second Hispanic concentration has developed in the Orlando metropolitan region. Here, many low wage jobs have been created within the region's huge tourist industry. Whereas Cubans are the largest Hispanic group on the Gold Coast, Puerto Ricans comprise the largest Hispanic group in the Orlando metropolitan area. Puerto Ricans are not only coming directly from Puerto Rico to the Orlando area, but many, including some of those who have retired, are arriving from elsewhere in the United States. Today, the Orlando area has become one of the nation's largest Puerto Rican enclaves.

Another sector of Florida's economy that has provided employment for Hispanics is agriculture. During the 1950s and 1960s, many Puerto Ricans were employed as migrant labor for the state's vegetable farms and citrus groves. In the 1980s, Mexicans began to replace Puerto Ricans. Lately, Guatemalans and

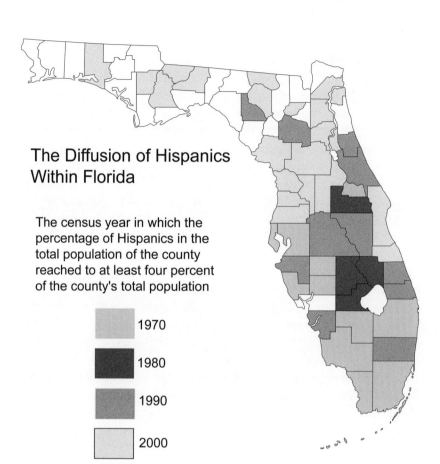

The Diffusion of Hispanics Within Florida

The census year in which the percentage of Hispanics in the total population of the county reached to at least four percent of the county's total population

1970

1980

1990

2000

Fig. 2.2. The diffusion of Hispanics.

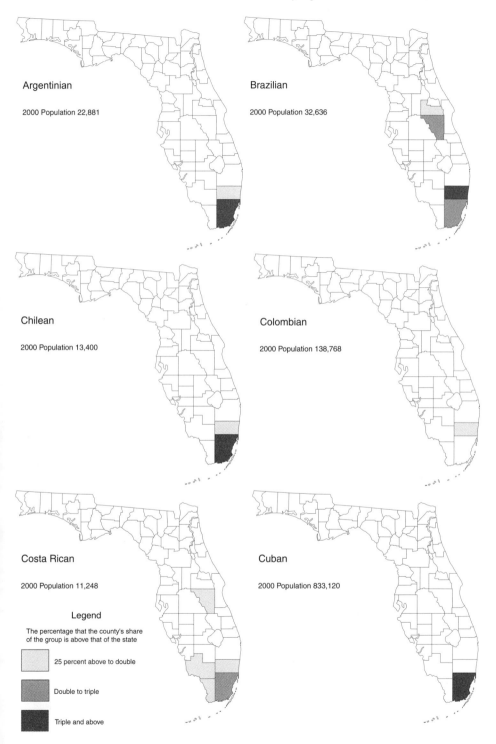

Argentinian

2000 Population 22,881

Brazilian

2000 Population 32,636

Chilean

2000 Population 13,400

Colombian

2000 Population 138,768

Costa Rican

2000 Population 11,248

Cuban

2000 Population 833,120

Legend

The percentage that the county's share
of the group is above that of the state

25 percent above to double

Double to triple

Triple and above

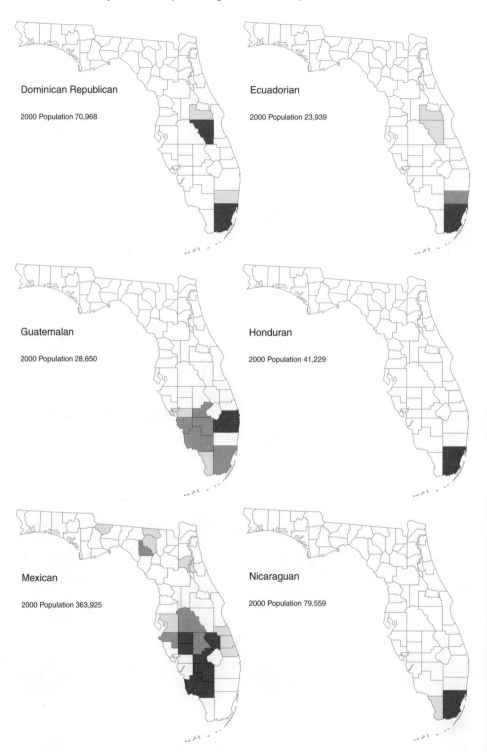

Dominican Republican

2000 Population 70,968

Ecuadorian

2000 Population 23,939

Guatemalan

2000 Population 28,650

Honduran

2000 Population 41,229

Mexican

2000 Population 363,925

Nicaraguan

2000 Population 79,559

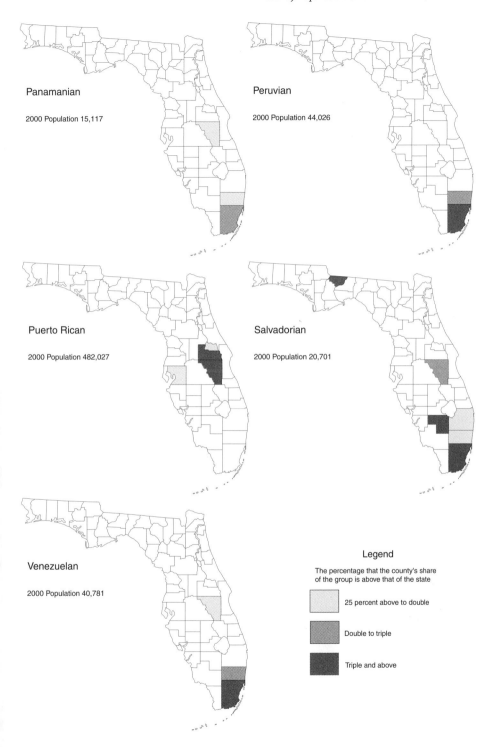

Panamanian

2000 Population 15,117

Peruvian

2000 Population 44,026

Puerto Rican

2000 Population 482,027

Salvadorian

2000 Population 20,701

Venezuelan

2000 Population 40,781

Legend

The percentage that the county's share
of the group is above that of the state

25 percent above to double

Double to triple

Triple and above

Salvadorans are arriving to work in agriculture. Many of the counties where shares of these three groups are considerably higher than their shares in the state's population are rural or, if urban, have an important agricultural sector. Indiantown, in Martin County, located just to the north of Palm Beach County, is said to have a larger Guatemalan Mayan Indian population than most Guatemalan towns.

Since many Hispanic agricultural workers in Florida are migratory, they do not form a permanent part of specific county populations. However, if they were living in a county on April 1, 2000—the day the nation's population was enumerated—they were counted as residents. Consequently, their place specificity may have resulted from an intensity of county agricultural activity in early April. Gadsden County provides a good example of this situation. At the time of the census, the number of Hispanics in residence in the county was relatively low, since many were working in the fields of South and Central Florida. There would have been many more had the census been taken in late spring or fall, seasons when the county is harvesting tomatoes. The problem that undocumented workers tend to avoid being enumerated also makes ascertaining the size of an immigrant population difficult.

By identifying the census at points when a county's Hispanic population reached 4 percent of its total, it is possible to see how this group has diffused throughout the state (fig. 2.1). The 1970 census was the first to identify Hispanics. In that year, Miami-Dade County's Hispanic population had reached 22 percent of the total, and Hillsborough's was 7 percent. During the 1960s, Hispanics, particularly Mexicans, began to be an important component of the state's agricultural labor force. As a result, their share in several rural counties in the southern half of the peninsula helped elevate those Hispanic populations to at least 4 percent. During the 1970s, Hispanics continued to enter Florida's agricultural workforce in large numbers, but others were attracted to Orange County (Orlando) where they filled service positions in the rapidly expanding tourist industry. The spillover of Hispanics from Miami-Dade County into nearby Broward (Ft. Lauderdale) during that decade was sufficient for that county's share of Hispanics to reach 4 percent. During the same period, the share of Hispanics in a number of rural counties on the peninsula also reached or surpassed that level. Between 1980 and 1990 more peninsular counties with important agriculture or tourism economies increased their shares of Hispanics to at least 4 percent. Between 1990 and 2000, Florida's Hispanics experienced their widest diffusion. In that decade, 22 counties, most of them in the northern half of the peninsula or in North Florida, acquired a sufficient number of Hispanics that their share reached the threshold to be included on the map. By then, Hispanics not only made up very important components of the labor force in urban services and agriculture, but also were disproportionately represented in construction, building and grounds maintenance, and forestry.

Other Western Hemisphere Ancestry

Most immigrants to Florida from non-Hispanic Western Hemisphere countries arrived from former French and English colonies in the Caribbean, particularly Haiti and Jamaica. These groups have had a long presence in Florida, but since the 1980s their populations in the state have risen dramatically. Most are black, and among them, many arrive in Florida poor and with little education. They mainly have settled on the peninsula, particularly its southern half. The Jamaicans and Bahamians have concentrations in fewer counties than the Haitians, the Trinidadians, and the Guyanese. The latter three have shares of the total population of several counties in the Orlando urban area that are exceptionally high compared to their shares within the state's population. The same is true of the Guyanese in the Tampa Bay area.

Most Canadians, whether they call themselves "Canadian" or "French Canadian," fit into four categories: (1) those who emigrated to the United States many years ago and spent their productive lives elsewhere in the nation, only retiring to Florida; (2) those who retired to Florida after spending their productive lives in Canada; (3) those who came to work in Florida; and (4) those who were vacationing in Florida on April 1, 2000, when the census was taken. The first group probably outnumbers the others, since the counties where Canadians have a significant presence conform closely to counties where the total non-Hispanic white retiree population also forms a large concentration. It is probable that many Canadians and French Canadians are retirees.

In the absence of a more logical place, this section has been chosen for the map depicting the by-county overrepresentation of respondents who identified their ancestry as American or "United States." This umbrella category covers all of those who identified their ancestry on the census form as "American" or by naming a state or national region (for example, "the South" or "New England"). The choice of "United States" ancestry has been particularly attractive to residents of counties in North Florida and the Peninsular Interior. Perhaps the reason is that within these counties the share of foreign-born is low, while the share of people who claim ancestry from somewhere in the British Isles is high. Because these original immigrants arrived in the United States

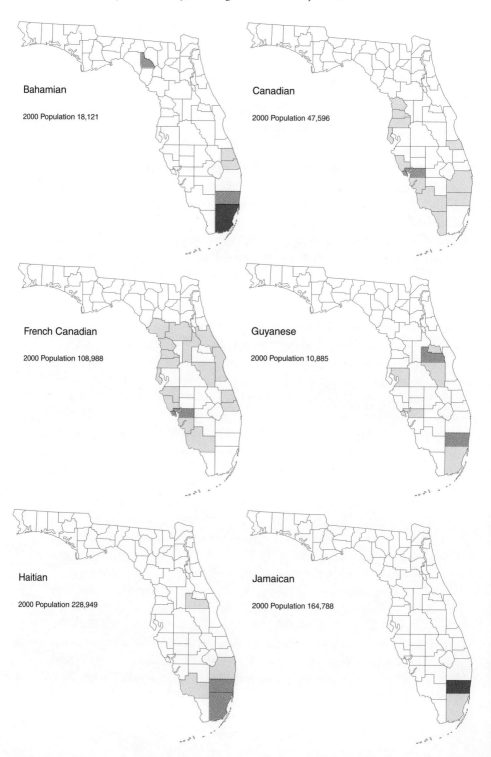

Bahamian

2000 Population 18,121

Canadian

2000 Population 47,596

French Canadian

2000 Population 108,988

Guyanese

2000 Population 10,885

Haitian

2000 Population 228,949

Jamaican

2000 Population 164,788

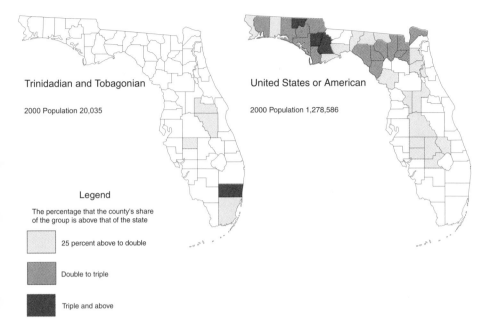

Trinidadian and Tobagonian

2000 Population 20,035

United States or American

2000 Population 1,278,586

Legend

The percentage that the county's share
of the group is above that of the state

25 percent above to double

Double to triple

Triple and above

many generations ago, perhaps some among the descendants have chosen to abandon recognition of their British heritage and simply accept their ancestry as "United States" or "American."

Although their numbers in Florida fall below 5,000 and do not warrant a map, the distribution of the state's Cajun population is interesting. More formally called Acadians, the Cajuns are descended from French Canadians who were resettled by the English from Nova Scotia in the middle of the eighteenth century. Many were sent to Louisiana where today they are highly concentrated to the west and south of New Orleans. They have gradually spread along the Gulf coast, and in 2000 1,990 were living in Florida. Not surprisingly, the Cajuns are overrepresented mainly in the Panhandle counties. Here live approximately 9 percent of all Floridians, but about one-third of the state's Cajuns. Escambia County (Pensacola) has 13 percent of the state's Cajuns, a share almost seven times higher than their share in the state's population. Walton County (DeFuniak Springs), Bay County (Panama City), Okaloosa County (Fort Walton Beach), Santa Rosa County (Milton), and Gulf County (Port St. Joe), all have at least three times the share of Cajuns in their populations as the state does.

European Ancestry

In the 2000 census, most Floridians chose their ancestry from among the European groups. Of those claiming European ancestry, only a small percentage were actually born in Europe. Among the latter, most were retirees who spent their productive years elsewhere in the United States, although a few may have (1) arrived in Florida in their youths, (2) retired to Florida after spending their productive lives in Europe, or (3) been visiting Florida on the day the census was levied. The majority of those who claimed European ancestry, however, descended from people who were born on that continent many generations ago. In fact, the European ancestry of a large number of Floridians has become so complicated over time that preference rather than proof probably motivated one or more of the respondents' choices.

Though the evidence is circumstantial, distribution similarities between counties with well-represented European groups in their total populations and counties where non-Hispanic white retirees are overrepresented support the supposition that many who claim European ancestry are also retired. Retired Finns have become especially well represented in Palm Beach County, and their share in the county's population is over three times their share in that of the state. Also, many Finns, both from the United States and Finland, have for decades vacationed in Palm Beach County, particularly in and around Lake Worth. In fact, the Finnish national airline Finnair used to put Lake Worth, not Miami, on maps accompanying their schedules, even though the latter was the true destination. Eventually, many Finns retired to the Lake Worth area, where they have established sauna societies and other Finnish cultural institutions.

Those who identified their ancestry in the census as Greek, Russian, and Yugoslavian also deserve special attention. Earlier it was mentioned that Greeks arrived in Florida at the beginning of the twentieth century, many coming to dive for sponges in the Keys. After disease reduced sponge harvests there, the Greeks resettled farther north, mainly along the Gulf Coast, particularly in Pinellas County. Here, especially in and around Tarpon Springs, they formed a relatively large enclave that exists today. It should be added that the Greek population in the Tarpon Springs area is a multigenerational rather than a heavily retired one. The Panhandle county of Franklin also attracted Greek fishermen early in the twentieth century; it continues to have a higher share of Greeks in its population than the state as a whole.

Russians have a huge presence in Florida, and most are Jewish. Scholars have long used Russian ancestry as a way to identify where Jews live in the United States, as so many are descended from people who once lived in the

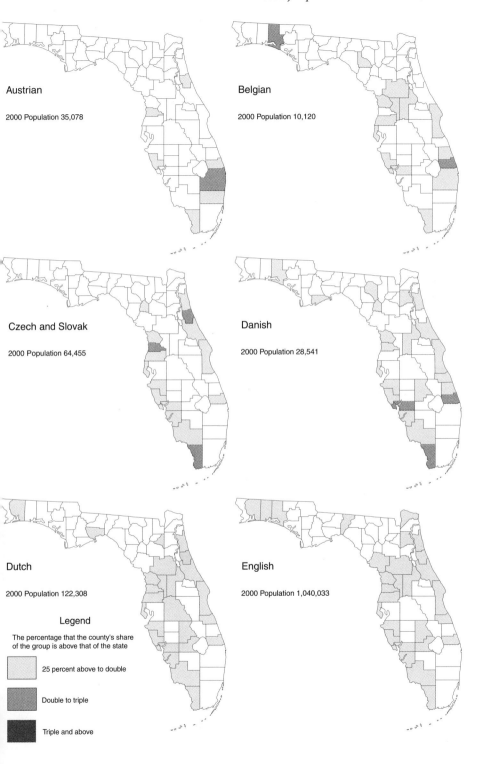

Austrian

2000 Population 35,078

Belgian

2000 Population 10,120

Czech and Slovak

2000 Population 64,455

Danish

2000 Population 28,541

Dutch

2000 Population 122,308

English

2000 Population 1,040,033

Legend

The percentage that the county's share
of the group is above that of the state

25 percent above to double

Double to triple

Triple and above

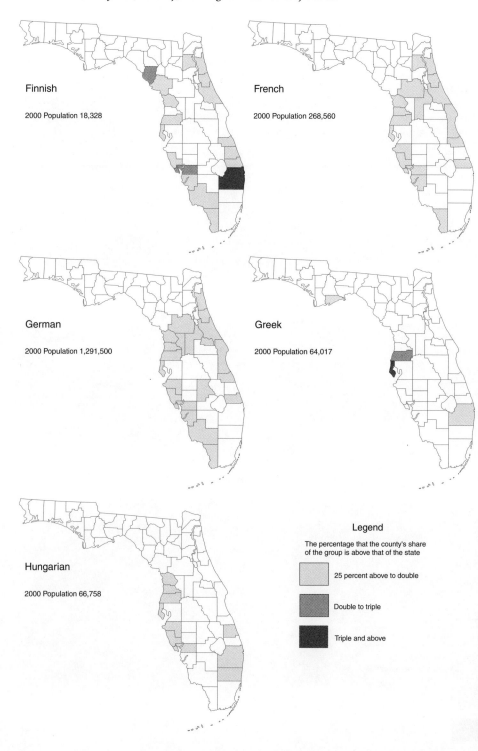

Finnish

2000 Population 18,328

French

2000 Population 268,560

German

2000 Population 1,291,500

Greek

2000 Population 64,017

Hungarian

2000 Population 66,758

Legend

The percentage that the county's share
of the group is above that of the state

25 percent above to double

Double to triple

Triple and above

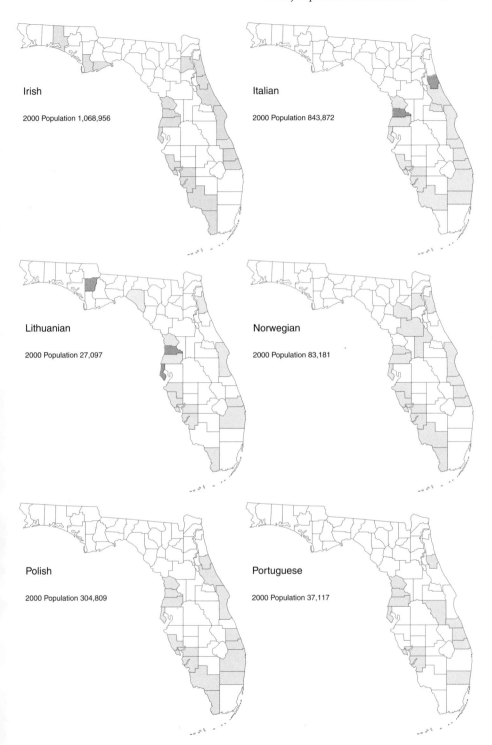

Irish

2000 Population 1,068,956

Italian

2000 Population 843,872

Lithuanian

2000 Population 27,097

Norwegian

2000 Population 83,181

Polish

2000 Population 304,809

Portuguese

2000 Population 37,117

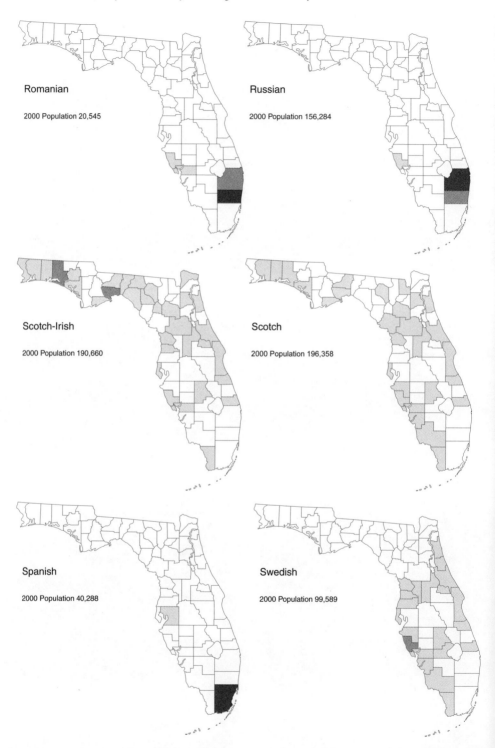

Romanian

2000 Population 20,545

Russian

2000 Population 156,284

Scotch-Irish

2000 Population 190,660

Scotch

2000 Population 196,358

Spanish

2000 Population 40,288

Swedish

2000 Population 99,589

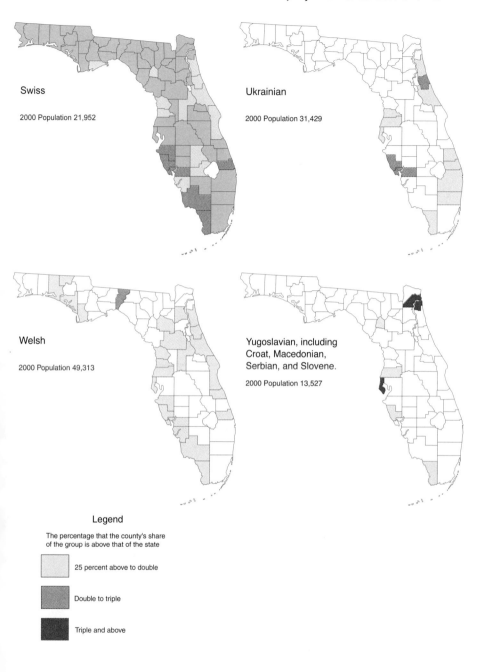

Swiss

2000 Population 21,952

Ukrainian

2000 Population 31,429

Welsh

2000 Population 49,313

Yugoslavian, including
Croat, Macedonian,
Serbian, and Slovene.

2000 Population 13,527

Legend

The percentage that the county's share
of the group is above that of the state

25 percent above to double

Double to triple

Triple and above

Russian Empire. The map shows that the share of Russians in the populations of Gold Coast counties is considerably higher than their share in the population of the state. Here, most are Jewish retirees. Until 1970, the greatest overrepresentation of Russians was in Miami-Dade County, particularly in the city of Miami Beach. With the arrival of the Hispanics, the Jews started moving to Broward County and shortly thereafter spread further north into Palm Beach County. While a smaller share of Austrians, Hungarians, and Romanians is Jewish, their distribution throughout the state is similar to the Russian distribution pattern.

Until 2000, Yugoslavians weren't overrepresented in any Florida county. In the 2000 census, however, they were overrepresented in Pinellas County (St. Petersburg) and Duval County (Jacksonville). During Yugoslavia's recent civil war, committees were formed in these counties to assist in the resettlement of Yugoslavian refugees, principally Croatians.

The distribution of counties where the Scotch-Irish are overrepresented helps define the location of "Old Florida"—that part of the state retaining much of its pre–World War II character. As the map indicates, counties with high concentrations of Scotch-Irish are mainly in the northern part of the state. North Florida during the territorial period attracted many immigrants of Scotch-Irish and Scotch ancestry from the Carolinas and Virginia. Since 1997, on one weekend in autumn, Leon County (Tallahassee) has held the Scottish Highland Games and Celtic Festival, which includes not only traditional games, but pipe bands, whisky tasting, a golf tournament, and a ceilidh dance in the evening. Regularly, about 30 Celtic clans and societies are represented. Though seldom so elaborate, Celtic festivals are also held elsewhere in the state.

Middle Eastern and African Ancestry

Middle Easterners have had a long presence in Florida. The first concentrations formed in Hillsborough County (Tampa) and Duval County (Jacksonville) early in the twentieth century. Today, the shares of Lebanese, Palestinians, and Syrians in Florida's population are actually higher than those of the nation. The first Middle Easterners to arrive were predominantly Christian, but today most newcomers from the region are Muslim. Although people from the Middle East continue to be unusually well represented in Duval County, today the Orlando and Gold Coast areas have developed especially large concentrations of people from this region. Alachua County (Gainesville) had unusually large shares of Egyptians, Iranians, and Turks in 2000. This is probably because Gainesville's University of Florida has more applied educational and

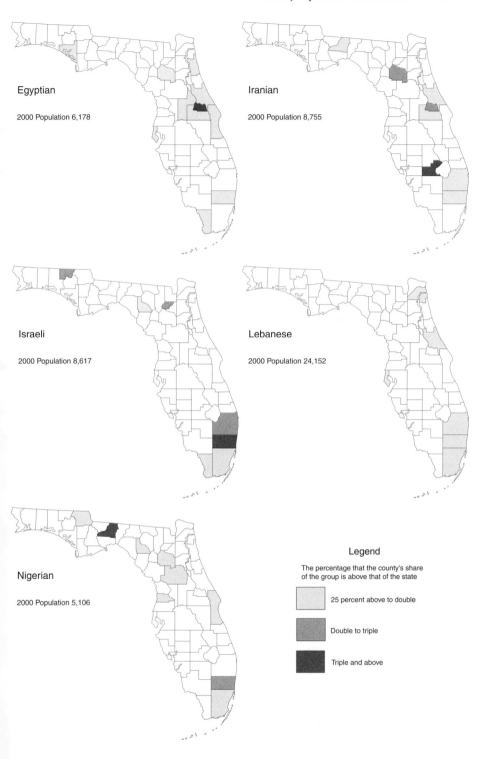

Egyptian

2000 Population 6,178

Iranian

2000 Population 8,755

Israeli

2000 Population 8,617

Lebanese

2000 Population 24,152

Nigerian

2000 Population 5,106

Legend

The percentage that the county's share
of the group is above that of the state

25 percent above to double

Double to triple

Triple and above

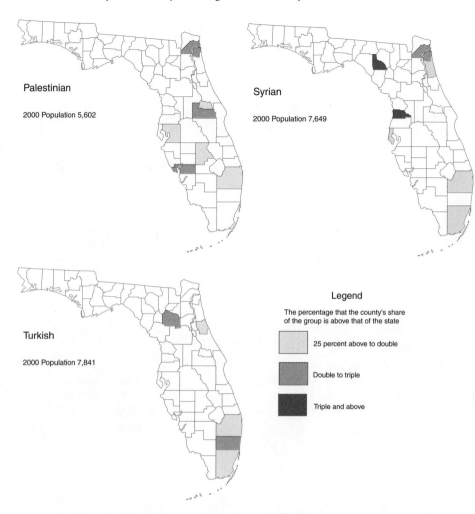

Palestinian

2000 Population 5,602

Syrian

2000 Population 7,649

Turkish

2000 Population 7,841

Legend

The percentage that the county's share
of the group is above that of the state

25 percent above to double

Double to triple

Triple and above

training programs than any other state higher educational institution and as a consequence has attracted students and faculty from these nations. The Orlando area, particularly Seminole County (Sanford), has a high concentration of Egyptians. Though the census does not differentiate Jewish Israelis from those who are Muslim or Christian, it is likely that the high Israeli concentration on the Gold Coast is mainly Jewish, as so many American Jews concentrate there as well.

Perhaps because of Florida's Southern heritage, few people of sub–Saharan African origin, most of them black, have chosen to live here. At the time of the 2000 census, Nigerians were the only group from sub-Saharan Africa that had a population in Florida that exceeded 5,000. Only a few counties had shares of Nigerians in their populations exceeding those of the state. Leon County's share, however, was over three times that of Florida. In part, the county's relatively large Nigerian population emerged because two large state universities are located in Tallahassee, and one is primarily black. A chain migration appears to have started during the 1960s, the original immigrants attracting others, some directly from Nigeria, some from elsewhere in the United States. Today, most of the county's Nigerians are no longer associated with its universities. Instead, they comprise a host of professions as civil servants, taxi drivers, physicians, small shop owners, retail sales personnel, and others. In 2004 a native Nigerian professor of public administration at Tallahassee Community College stood (unsuccessfully) for election to that city's commission. Another resident, John Agwunobi, whose father was born in Nigeria, at the time of writing was the state's Secretary of Health.

Other Asian Ancestry

Longtime Florida residents might assume, as they observe the proliferation of Chinese, Thai, Vietnamese, and Asian Indian restaurants throughout the state, that Florida is being inundated by Asians. Tallahassee, for instance, had no Chinese restaurants in 1965, but by 2005 hosted over twenty. Many of the state's smaller rural towns now have at least one. Actually, compared to many states, particularly California, people from the Far East and the Indian Subcontinent have not found in Florida a very attractive destination. The percentage of Chinese in the state's population is 66 percent lower than that of the nation. For Koreans and Japanese, the figure is even lower. Nonetheless, during the 1990s, Florida's population from the Far East and the Indian Subcontinent increased substantially, although not evenly, throughout the state.

Alachua County (Gainesville) has been particularly attractive to Asians of many origins, including Asian Indians, Chinese, Koreans, Japanese, Pakistanis, Thais, and Vietnamese. The share of Chinese, Koreans, and Japanese in the total population of Leon County (Tallahassee) also markedly exceeds that of the state. As noted earlier, both Alachua and Leon counties house major universities that have attracted students and scholars from these nations. Two counties in the Orlando area also have drawn, at least by Florida standards, a greater number of Asian people than might be expected given the size of their populations. Pakistanis not only have found the Orlando area especially inviting but the Gold Coast as well. Filipinos have an extraordinarily large presence in the Jacksonville and Pensacola areas, a reflection of their long and deep involvement with the U.S. Navy, which maintains large bases there.

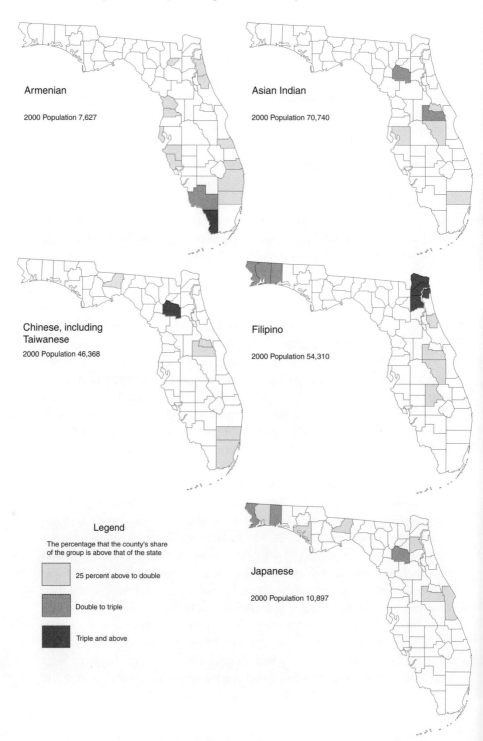

Armenian

2000 Population 7,627

Asian Indian

2000 Population 70,740

Chinese, including
Taiwanese

2000 Population 46,368

Filipino

2000 Population 54,310

Legend

The percentage that the county's share
of the group is above that of the state

25 percent above to double

Double to triple

Triple and above

Japanese

2000 Population 10,897

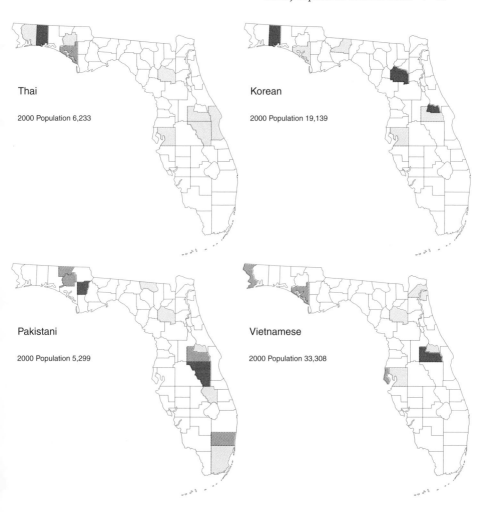

Thai

2000 Population 6,233

Korean

2000 Population 19,139

Pakistani

2000 Population 5,299

Vietnamese

2000 Population 33,308

Vietnamese also are overrepresented by Florida standards in several coastal counties: Escambia (Pensacola), Duval (Jacksonville), Bay (Panama City), Pinellas (St. Petersburg), and Hillsborough (Tampa). Following the end of the Vietnam War, many Vietnamese fled their homeland. Although most chose to live in California, many settled in ports along the Gulf of Mexico where they frequently work in fishing. Although coastal Florida counties have large concentrations of this group, the largest concentration is found in Orange County (Orlando), situated in Florida's interior. While the reason is unclear, it is worthy to note the paucity of Florida coastal counties where people from India are overrepresented. The Pakistanis, however, are overrepresented in both Broward and Miami-Dade counties.

Ancestry Diversity

As of the 2000 census, counties with large populations unsurprisingly had more ancestry groups overrepresented in their total populations compared to their share in the state's population than counties with smaller populations (fig. 2.3). The Gold Coast's three counties, all with over one million inhabitants, together form the state's most cosmopolitan region. In 2000, over half (51 percent) of the 81 ancestry groups identified in this atlas were overrepresented in Broward County's population, 42 percent in Miami-Dade County's population, and 31 percent in Palm Beach County's population. Other Florida counties with large cities also had many groups that were overrepresented, among them Pinellas (St. Petersburg) and Orange (Orlando).

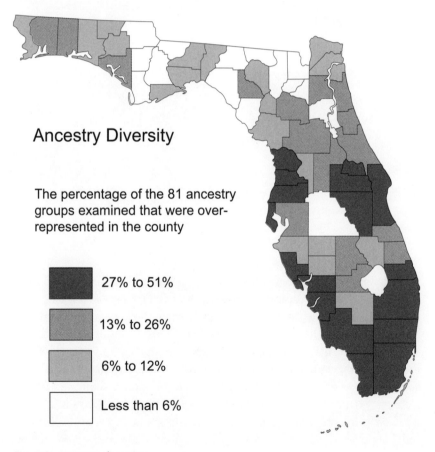

Fig. 2.3. Ancestry diversity.

The cultural diversity of the Gold Coast is well represented by the South Florida *Sun-Sentinel*'s "Multicultural Directory" that supplies cultural, business, educational, government, legal, civic, and political information oriented to specific cultural groups (http://southflorida.sun- sentinel.com/news/multicultural/). The directory cites well over 150 cultural institutions, and even includes groups with diverse sexual orientations. As one would expect, the Alliance Francaise and American German Club are included, but so are Drums of Polynesia, the Ashanti Cultural Arts Association, and the Akwa Ibom Association formed by Nigerians of Ibo ancestry. In fact, there are at least three other clubs for different Nigerian tribes. The directory also lists 42 festivals celebrating cultural diversity. The most famous among them is the Calle Ocho, a ten-day celebration sponsored by the Kiwanis Club of Little Havana which aims to promote "community spirit" and to benefit "youth with scholarships, educational, sports, and outreach programs." Similarly, the mission of the Thai Asian Festival is to "promote and develop Thai culture," while the Cajun Zydeco Crawfish Festival promotes "the Cajun Zydeco culture of Louisiana." These are just a few of many.

Several counties with relatively small populations also have highly diverse populations. They include Monroe (Key West), Highlands (Avon Park), and Flagler County (Palm Coast). Flagler County's remarkably complex population deserves elaboration. Until the 1970s it was a lightly populated, primarily agricultural county that fronted on the Atlantic Ocean. A large corporation purchased waterfront land to develop what they named Palm Coast. Today the more than 40,000 people living in this ancestrally diverse community make up a two-thirds share of the county's population. The developers have been highly successful in attracting an incredibly diverse population. Most ancestry groups that are highly overrepresented in Flagler County are European, especially Italians, Czechs, and Ukrainians. However, Turks, Armenians, and Filipinos, among others from Asia and the Pacific also are unusually well represented, along with several others. It should be remembered that for ancestry groups with small populations to be overrepresented, it does not take many members in a county with as small a population as that of Flagler.

A few counties with populations that in 2000 exceeded 250,000 had relatively few overrepresented ancestry groups. The largest among them were Hillsborough (Tampa), Duval (Jacksonville), Polk (Lakeland), and Escambia (Pensacola). These and most other counties with low percentages of overrepresented population groups neither greatly appeal to retirees nor enjoy tourist-driven economies. Consequently, they are growing at a relatively slow rate. Several counties with this profile are located in North Florida where the economy is heavily oriented toward agriculture and forestry.

3

A Brief History of Religion in Florida

Two Spanish Periods and the British Interlude

The Spanish brought Christianity to Florida early in the sixteenth century. In 1539 the first Christmas mass in what is today the United States was celebrated at the temporary encampment of Hernando de Soto's exploratory party, located on the site of today's Tallahassee. Throughout the first Spanish period, which ended in 1763, the monarchy permitted only Catholic worship and worked vigorously to convert the Indians to that religion. First the Jesuits were invited to establish missions among the Indians. Later the Franciscans replaced the Jesuits and built a string of missions between St. Augustine—seat of the colonial government of East Florida—and the Apalachicola River. Here they gathered the Indians not only for religious instruction, but also to teach them European technology with the partial intention of producing agricultural surpluses to supply St. Augustine. At the beginning of the eighteenth century, these missions were destroyed by the English who arrived with their Indian allies from South Carolina to capture mission Indians to work as slaves on Carolinian plantations.

Between 1763 and 1783, England gained possession of the colony. During its short reign, the English built the first Protestant houses of worship, all Church of England. The English, however, *did* permit Catholics to maintain their own churches, and in at least one case (New Smyrna) authorized the establishment of a new Catholic congregation. Most Spaniards, as well as some Indians who had converted to Catholicism, left for other Spanish colonies, particularly Cuba or Spain. Following the departure of the English and the reestablishment of Spanish rule, public observance of any religion other than Catholicism was once again prohibited. The Spanish governor, however, in an effort to populate the colony, ignored the prohibition and permitted the Protestants who remained, as well as those who moved in from the new southern states, to engage in discrete worship. Most Protestants at this time were Episcopal, Methodist, Baptist, or Presbyterian.

Territorial Period until 1950

In 1821 Florida became a U.S. territory and immediately began to attract immigrants, mostly Protestants from the southern states. There is considerable debate as to which Protestant denomination was the first to establish a congregation in the new territory. During the 1820s, Episcopal, Methodist, Baptist, and Presbyterian congregations were established in several parts of the Florida territory. Few had permanent preachers and were serviced instead by "circuit riders." An estimated 500 to 750 Catholics, most in and around St. Augustine and Pensacola, remained in Florida following the departure of the Spanish. However, it was not until well into the 1830s that these congregations had permanent priests.

Plantation owners were active in converting their slaves to their religions and provided segregated sections for them within plantation-based places of worship. After the Civil War and emancipation, blacks formed their own religious conferences, most notably the African Methodist Episcopal Church. Most blacks today, however, worship in churches independent of, or only loosely affiliated with, older denominations.

Jews first arrived in Florida during the English period, but it was only during the territorial period that they took significant part in Florida's political and economic affairs. In 1845, David Levy became the first Jew ever to serve in the United States Senate. The first Jewish congregation was formed in Pensacola in 1874. Until the latter part of the nineteenth century, few Catholics arrived in Florida to reinvigorate the small number descended from those who lived there at the time Spain ceded its colony to the United States.

During the last third of the nineteenth century, immigration to Florida increased. More people began to arrive from U.S. locations other than the South. In addition, the number of foreign immigrants grew. The long and violent revolution against Spanish colonial rule in Cuba brought many exiles from that island, first to Key West, and later to Tampa and to a lesser degree to Jacksonville. Virtually all were Catholic. Tampa also received Italian Catholics during the last decades of the nineteenth century. Nonetheless, as late as 1906, only 17,507 Catholics were enumerated in the whole state. Baptists, who by 1906 had replaced the Methodists as the Florida denomination with the most members, held a 42-percent share of the state's church membership, while Methodists held a 37-percent share. The Catholics occupied third place with 9 percent; the Episcopalians fourth place, with 4 percent; and the Presbyterians fifth place, with 3 percent. The remaining 5 percent of church members were scattered mainly among Adventists, Congregationalists, and Disciples of Christ. In 1906, the religious configuration of Florida closely resembled that of other southeastern states.

After World War I, the southern half of Florida experienced a tremendous land boom ignited by wildly inflated prospects of tourism and tropical agriculture. The boom brought not only southerners—long the most important source of new citizens—but also people from the North, who greatly increased the state's religious diversity. The religion census of 1936 identified Florida's five largest denominations not only as the same ones identified in 1906, but in the same order. Taken together, however, these five in 1936 held only an 85-percent share of the state's church members compared to 95 percent in 1906. The sixth largest religious group that year was the Jewish, with 18,769 members. The Disciples of Christ had 9,527 members, and the Adventists and Churches of Christ had approximately 6,000 each. Denominations that were not traditionally southern began to appear in the census. It might be added that in 1936 the neighboring states of Georgia and Alabama continued to have roughly 95 percent of their church members within their five leading denominations, just as they did in 1906.

Post–World War II Period

The world depression of the 1930s, followed by World War II, slowed population growth in Florida. Following World War II, growth resumed at a pace far more rapid than before the war. Furthermore, people increasingly arrived in Florida from outside the South. Jews in particular, many of them retirees, formed a significant share of the migration. Today, the Jewish religion is the fourth largest in the state, and the state's Jewish population ranks as the third largest in the nation. Except for the United States and Israel, Florida's Jewish population exceeds that of any nation.

Beginning in the 1960s, economic and social unrest spread throughout the Caribbean Basin, including Central America, Colombia, and Venezuela. Florida became a major destination for people from that region, most of them Catholic. By the 1970s, more people in the state identified with Catholicism than with any other religion. The second largest denomination at that time was the Baptist, followed by the Methodist, Jewish, and Episcopal. As in 1936, adherents of the five leading state religions held an 85–percent share of all the state's religious adherents. However, a number of religions that weren't even identified in the 1936 census comprised the remaining 15 percent. These included the Eastern religions of Islam, Hinduism, and Buddhism. Also important to the proliferation of religions in Florida was the creation of new denominations from older ones as the result of doctrinal schisms, a subject that will be discussed later.

4

Contemporary Distribution
of Religious Denominations in Florida

Introduction

Although the U.S. Census Bureau conducted its last religion census almost 70 years ago, the Glenmary Home Missioners research center has filled the breach by gathering data on religious denominations in 1952, 1971, 1980, 1990, and 2000. Adding denominations with each successive study, the most recent census represented 149 denominations out of 285 queried. Regrettably, at least 14 with an estimated 100,000 adherents did not respond, and many of these nonresponsive denominations were black. Martin Luther King once observed that the most segregated hour in the nation is 11 o'clock on Sunday morning. Although this is merely an observation, research has shown that most U.S. congregations are not multiracial. Consequently, readers should remember that denominational data contained in this atlas largely represent a limited selection of Florida's white congregations. Despite its deficiencies, however, the center's census is the only one that provides religious data at the county level.

The 2000 Glenmary denominational census identified that a far lower share of Florida's white population professed religious affiliation than that of the nation. For Florida, the share was 52 percent, while for the nation it was 65 percent. Florida's neighbors had much larger shares: Georgia's was 68 percent, and Alabama's was 76 percent. It is not clear why Florida's share is so low. Its fast growth could be a contributing factor. Coincidentally or not, two states with much smaller populations than Florida, but with high rates of population growth, also show shares of non-adherents in their populations comparable to those of Florida: Arizona at 51 percent and Nevada at only 44 percent. On the other hand, California and Texas—states with similarly rapid growth over the past few decades—have shares far higher than Florida.

Compared to that of the entire nation, Florida has a far higher share of religious adherents who identify with the Assembly of God, the Churches of God (Cleveland, TN), the Episcopal Church, the Greek Orthodox Church, the Pentecostal Holiness Church, the Presbyterian Church in America, the Seventh-day Adventists, the Baptists affiliated with the Southern Baptist Con-

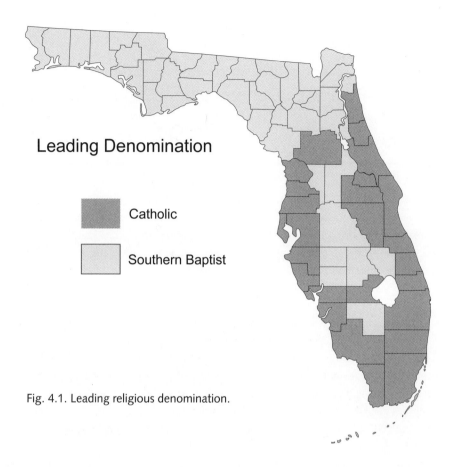

Fig. 4.1. Leading religious denomination.

vention (hereafter called Southern Baptists), and with Judaism. The shares of adherents within the Church of Jesus Christ of Latter-day Saints (Mormons), the Disciples of Christ, the Evangelical Lutheran Church in America and the Lutheran Church (Missouri Synod), the United Church of Christ, and the Muslims, are much lower than their shares within the total for the nation.

All 67 counties in 2000 reported that either Southern Baptists or Roman Catholics comprised their two largest denominations (fig. 4:1). Southern Baptists predominated in Florida's northern and interior peninsular counties, most with markedly slower rates of population growth than those along the peninsular coasts. Every coastal county from St. Johns around the Keys and up to Citrus County on the west coast has a Catholic majority. In the interior of the peninsula, Marion County (Ocala), Orange County (Orlando), and the two counties to the north and south of Orange County (Seminole

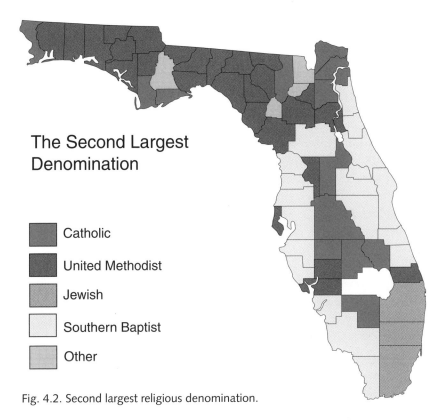

The Second Largest
Denomination

- Catholic
- United Methodist
- Jewish
- Southern Baptist
- Other

Fig. 4.2. Second largest religious denomination.

and Osceola) also now have Catholic majorities, as does Glades County on Lake Okeechobee. Most Catholic majority counties have experienced large immigrations, often from Latin America. Catholics comprise the second largest denomination in most counties with Southern Baptist majorities, and the reverse is true where Catholics dominate (fig. 4.2). In the northern part of the state, however, Methodists take second place to Southern Baptists, while on the Gold Coast, Jews follow Catholics in frequency.

Although the Southern Baptists experienced numeric growth during the 1990s, the growth in the number of Catholics was so great that their share of the state's total adherents increased by nine percentage points. This increase in relative importance or share of Catholics occurred at the expense of ten of Florida's major denominations, particularly the Baptists and Methodists. Since 1990 only one Protestant denomination, the Churches of God (Cleveland, TN), has been able to increase its share of the state's total adherents. While throughout the United States smaller Protestant denominations, many Pentecostal, have been enjoying great increase in their adherents, their share of total adherents in Florida actually declined between 1990 and 2000.

The growth in the share of Catholics among total adherents is largely attributed to the continuing flow of Hispanics into the state. The share decline in so many of the other denominations is due to the fact that their numbers depend largely on natural increase, while they receive few adherents from other states or from abroad. On the other hand, as table 4.1 reveals, most denominations actually grew in number of adherents between 1990 and 2000, or their number remained stable. Numerically, the greatest loss was experienced by the Presbyterian Church (USA). In large part that loss resulted from a schism that developed within the church between those who took a liberal stance on issues such as social justice and peace and those who took a more conservative view. This has led to the establishment of the more conservative Presbyterian Church in America.

The decline in the share of religious adherents in many of Florida's Protestant denominations may result from an overcount of Catholics by the Glenmary Research Center. Many who have arrived from Latin America, particularly from Central America, converted from Catholicism to Protestantism in their home countries, but might have been enumerated as Catholic when they arrived here; others have converted since they arrived. It is well known that among the Protestant denominations the Pentecostal religions have attracted the most adherents. Some evidence of the inroads of Protestantism among Hispanics, as well as among Haitians living in the Miami area, may be found in the proliferation of Protestant churches in Miami-Dade County, now over half Hispanic and with a large Haitian population. There are today at least ten Pentecostal churches in the relatively few blocks that constitute the core of Little Havana and well over one hundred scattered elsewhere throughout the county, including Little Haiti. Many other denominations now announce services in Spanish. Elsewhere throughout Florida the same phenomenon is taking place.

A high degree of religious diversity within Florida's counties is rare. Actually, only eight counties count fewer than half of their adherents within their top two denominations (fig. 4:3). All but Leon (Tallahassee) are rural with small populations. The three heavily populated Gold Coast counties (Miami-Dade, Broward, and Palm Beach) have a surprisingly smaller number of denominations than their populations would predict. This probably results from

Table 4.1. Major Florida religious denominations (number of adherents)

Denominations	1971	1971%	1980	1980%	1990	1990%	2000	2000%
Assembly of God	ND	ND	85,687	2	134,297	3	189,387	3
Catholic	917,458	31	1,353,478	34	1,598,457	32	2,596,148	41
Christian churches and Churches of Christ	25,461	1	33,139	1	43,070	1	58,695	1
Church of Christ (Disciples)	24,491	1	26,147	1	23,725	*	22,545	*
Church of Jesus Christ of Latter-day Saints	24,414	1	36,859	1	59,845	1	75,620	1
Church of the Nazarene	25,952	1	28,903	1	39,413	1	44,208	1
Churches of Christ	22,333	1	26,147	1	73,462	1	72,540	1
Churches of God (Cleveland, TN)	34,702	1	43,386	1	70,108	1	101,188	2
Episcopal Church	150,457	5	145,443	4	158,595	3	152,526	2
Evangelical Lutheran Churches in America	62,874	2	73,078	2	92,732	2	90,594	1
Greek Orthodox	ND	ND	ND	ND	ND	ND	24,796	*
Jewish estimate (American Jewish Committee)	269,620	9	452,000	12	567,000	11	628,458	10
Lutheran Church (Missouri Synod)	49,940	2	58,949	2	67,787	1	71,970	1
Muslim (Islam)	ND	ND	ND	ND	ND	ND	31,661	*
Pentecostal Holiness	4,944	*	8,711	*	11,815	*	27,907	*
Presbyterian Church (USA)	116,705	4	104,523	3	165,255	3	157,751	2
Presbyterian Church in America	ND	ND	17,726	*	35,998	1	43,745	1
Seventh-day Adventists	22,129	1	32,892	1	57,336	1	72,619	1
Southern Baptist Convention	806,190	27	937,719	24	1,167,850	23	1,292,097	20
United Church of Christ	39,805	1	32,709	1	43,854	1	39,326	1
United Methodist Church	385,051	13	426,591	11	462,174	9	458,623	7
Independent Charismatic churches	ND	ND	ND	ND	35,202	1	34,325	1
Independent non-Charismatic churches	ND	ND	ND	ND	84,048	2	57,243	1
Total adherents	2,982,526	100	3,924,087	100	4,992,023	100	6,343,994	100

Note: ND=No data or insufficient data.

* is less than 1/2 percent.

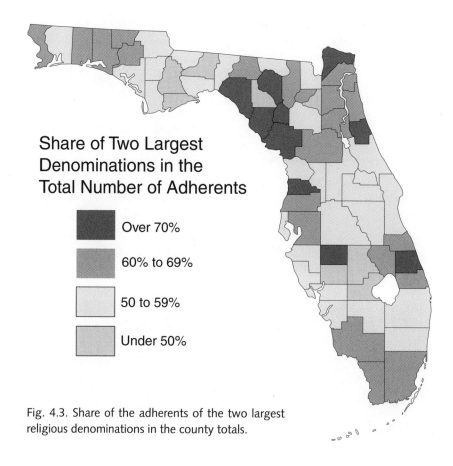

Fig. 4.3. Share of the adherents of the two largest
religious denominations in the county totals.

the dominance of Catholics and Jews whose combined presence in the Gold
Coast counties is enormous.

Contemporary Concentrations of Denominations

Maps have been drawn to identify those counties where the major denominations are most highly overrepresented within the state. That is, where the
county's share of a denomination among its total number of adherents is at
least 25 percent higher than the state's share of the denomination among all
of its religious adherents. The reader is once again reminded that these data
primarily represent white denominations, as many black denominations did
not participate in the Glenmary survey.

As suggested in earlier chapters, Florida logically can be divided into two
broad cultural regions, Old and New Florida. Old Florida has experienced

far less immigration than New Florida. As a result, compared with the white population of New Florida, that of Old Florida is more closely identified with religions that have long been important in the South. Several maps in the atlas help define Old Florida. Perhaps most useful is the one that depicts the counties where respondents claiming "United States" ancestry are disproportionately well represented in the total population. The counties that form New Florida are the fast growing ones on the peninsula's coasts and the interior peninsular counties with their large cities and suburbs.

When Florida joined the United States, people from the southeastern states, mainly the Carolinas, were first to arrive. Most who came were Baptist, Methodist, and Presbyterian. Even today, the distribution of Methodists and Presbyterians in the southeastern United States is regionally concentrated in two main areas: one in the Carolinas and one in Florida. Baptists, on the other hand, are more uniformly distributed throughout the South. Florida counties where the shares of Baptists, Methodists, and Presbyterians are far higher than the state average are commonly located in the northern and interior peninsular parts of the state.

Smaller Protestant denominations also have become well established in Old Florida. Variously originating in both the early nineteenth and early twentieth centuries, some in the southern states and others in the Midwest and even New England, most are intent on "purifying" Baptist and Methodist forms of Protestantism. Often evangelical and theologically conservative, many of the small Protestant denominations variously include ritual practices such as divine healing, speaking in tongues, baptism by total emersion, foot washing, and the prohibition of instrumental music during services. Not surprisingly, most of these newer Protestant denominations are overrepresented in the adherent populations of counties where Baptists comprise the largest denomination.

The newer Protestant denominations now firmly planted in the counties of North Florida and the interior peninsula include the Assembly of God, the Church of God (Cleveland, TN), and the Pentecostal Holiness Church. Those whose popularity is mainly confined to North Florida are the Church of Jesus Christ of Latter-day Saints (Mormons) and the Churches of Christ. In the peninsular interior, the Christian Churches and Churches of Christ, the Church of the Nazarene, the Seventh-day Adventists, and the Christian Church (Disciples of Christ) are unusually well represented. The Assembly of God is especially closely identified with the western Panhandle.

Catholics comprise the largest denomination in most New Florida counties. However, their share in Florida's total adherent population is now so large and so many live in the state's southeastern counties that only eight counties have shares of Catholics that are at least 25 percent above the state average. Hispanics and retirees from the northeastern states form a very large share of the Catholic population. Catholics are also well represented in Hardee and Hernando counties. Hardee, situated in the state's interior, has a heavily agricultural economy, and Mexicans and Central Americans compose most of the labor force. Hernando, located on the west coast, has attracted many non-Hispanic retirees to its retirement developments, a large share from northeastern states. Hernando County's share of people of Italian ancestry is over three times the share of this group in the state's population. One liberal Protestant denomination, the United Church of Christ, is especially popular among non-Hispanic whites on the Sun and Space coasts.

Two of Florida's larger denominations, the Lutheran and Presbyterian, have weathered theological schisms that produced newer denominations. The more conservative branch of the Lutherans, the Lutheran Church (Missouri Synod), is especially well represented among religious adherents in Old Florida counties. By contrast, the more liberal branch, the Evangelical Lutheran Churches in America, is well represented among religious adherents in New Florida counties. The two branches of the Presbyterian tree are the older, more liberal Presbyterian Church (USA) and the more conservative Presbyterian Church in America. In Florida, the Presbyterian schism has sometimes resulted in whole congregations converting from the USA to the America branch church. The distribution of the two Presbyterian denominations among Old and New Florida counties is not as clear as it is for the two Lutheran denominations. Nonetheless, adherents of the Presbyterian Church (USA) are especially well represented in peninsular counties; those of the Presbyterian Church in America are more visible in North Florida; and the two coexist in Leon County (Tallahassee). Recently, the issue of the ordination of gay ministers has widened the fissure between the liberal and conservative wings of the Presbyterian Church and threatens to split the Episcopal and Methodist churches as well. If the latter two denominations divide, it will be interesting to see whether or not they do so along Old Florida/New Florida lines.

Jews, as noted earlier, have become densely concentrated in Florida. Over 80 percent of the state's Jewish population lives in the three Gold Coast counties of Miami-Dade, Broward, and Palm Beach, where many are retirees. Within these three counties, moreover, Jews have further concentrated within relatively few communities. Good examples of towns where Jews have become important elements within their populations are Boca Raton and Delray Beach in Palm Beach County and Fort Lauderdale in Broward. Before the huge Latin American immigration to Miami-Dade County, Miami Beach's Jewish retiree population was so large that it became nationally famous, the subject of many movie and television productions and numerous jokes. Today its Jewish population has dwindled dramatically. Smaller, but substantial numbers of Jews, however, are found in all of Florida's large metropolitan areas.

The 2000 Glenmary religion census was the first to enumerate Muslims. At that time, an estimated 31,661 Muslims lived in Florida. Some were African-Americans, but most were recent arrivals from the Middle East. All were disproportionately well represented in counties with large cities. Probably as a result of their association with institutions of higher learning, Muslim shares of the religious adherents in Alachua County (University of Florida) and Leon County (Florida State University and Florida Agricultural and Mechanical University) were considerably higher than their share in the state's total Muslim adherent population.

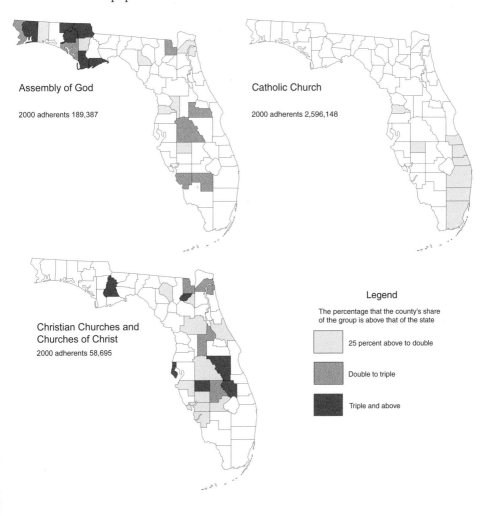

Assembly of God

2000 adherents 189,387

Catholic Church

2000 adherents 2,596,148

Christian Churches and
Churches of Christ
2000 adherents 58,695

Legend

The percentage that the county's share
of the group is above that of the state

25 percent above to double

Double to triple

Triple and above

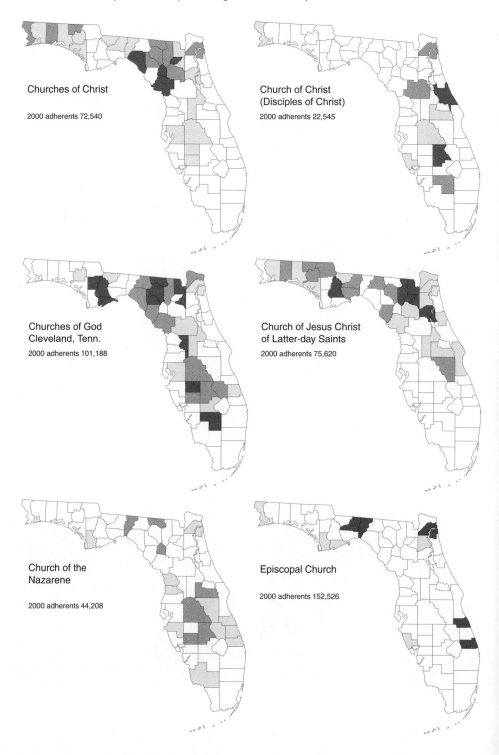

Churches of Christ

2000 adherents 72,540

Church of Christ
(Disciples of Christ)

2000 adherents 22,545

Churches of God
Cleveland, Tenn.

2000 adherents 101,188

Church of Jesus Christ
of Latter-day Saints

2000 adherents 75,620

Church of the
Nazarene

2000 adherents 44,208

Episcopal Church

2000 adherents 152,526

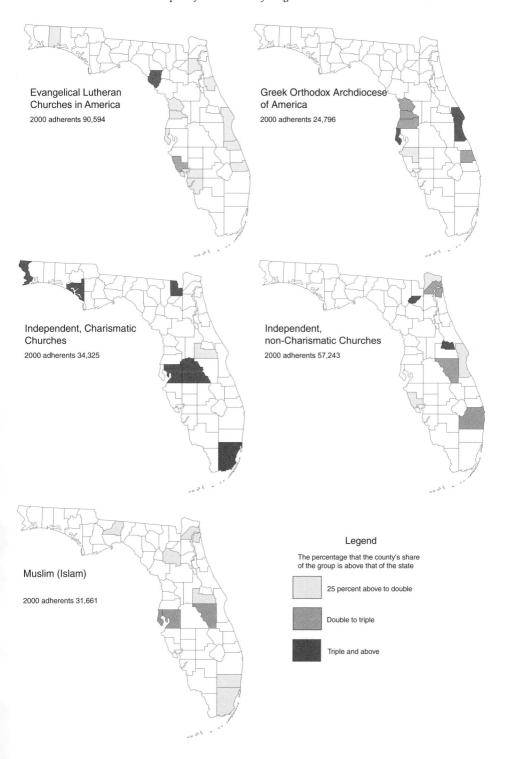

Evangelical Lutheran
Churches in America

2000 adherents 90,594

Greek Orthodox Archdiocese
of America

2000 adherents 24,796

Independent, Charismatic
Churches

2000 adherents 34,325

Independent,
non-Charismatic Churches

2000 adherents 57,243

Muslim (Islam)

2000 adherents 31,661

Legend

The percentage that the county's share
of the group is above that of the state

25 percent above to double

Double to triple

Triple and above

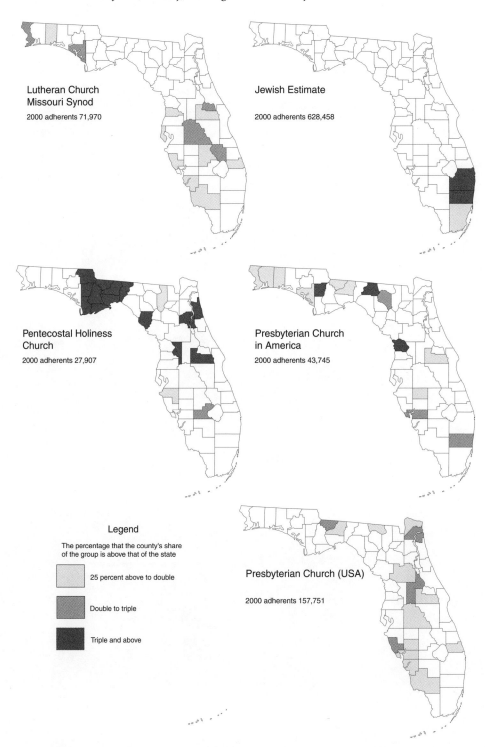

Lutheran Church
Missouri Synod

2000 adherents 71,970

Jewish Estimate

2000 adherents 628,458

Pentecostal Holiness
Church

2000 adherents 27,907

Presbyterian Church
in America

2000 adherents 43,745

Legend

The percentage that the county's share
of the group is above that of the state

25 percent above to double

Double to triple

Triple and above

Presbyterian Church (USA)

2000 adherents 157,751

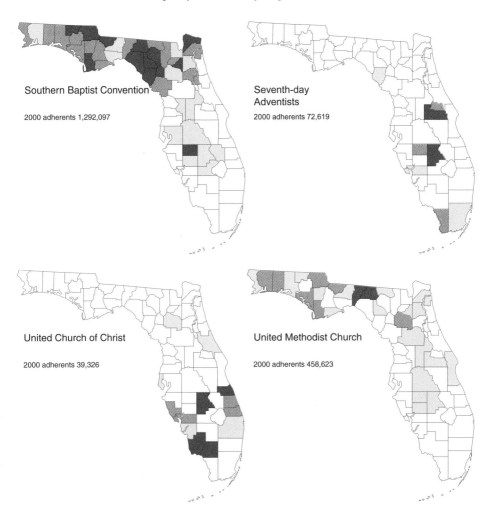

Southern Baptist Convention

2000 adherents 1,292,097

Seventh-day
Adventists

2000 adherents 72,619

United Church of Christ

2000 adherents 39,326

United Methodist Church

2000 adherents 458,623

5

Racial and Ancestry Distributions within Florida's Large Urban Areas

Introduction

Maps that show the geographic distribution of selected racial and ancestry groups within Florida's four largest urban areas have been drawn using U.S. Census tract data. Tracts are census units that typically have approximately 5,000 to 6,000 inhabitants. They are invaluable in identifying where people of different races and ancestry live within a given urban area. Here, distributions are shown using dot distribution maps. One dot represents a specific number of people within a group, the number varying according to the size of the group. While dot distribution maps are the most accurate means to identify the location of a population, they remain only approximations of distributions. Because the location of each dot depends upon the amount of the population within a tract, a great deal of dot overlap appears in some tracts. No dot appears in tracts that have fewer members of a group than one dot equals.

America's ethnic neighborhoods began to form early in the nineteenth century: the Irish neighborhoods of Boston and New York provide good examples. They became both larger and more numerous between 1880 and 1930, a period of massive European immigration. Economic activities in the nation's cities during that time were highly centralized as were their populations. The major destination of public transportation was the central business district, and surrounding it were factories as well as cheap housing for their workers, many of whom were recent immigrants from Europe. Since they could better provide social support to newcomers, ethnic neighborhoods formed at the centers of many large cities. Thus, we inherited the "littles" and the "towns": Little Italy, Little Athens, Little Warsaw, Little Bohemia, Germantown, and Chinatown.

For those who search today within the nation's large cities for European ethnic neighborhoods, like those portrayed in films such as the *Godfather*, their efforts, except in rare instances, will largely be in vain. In most cities, however, large areas remain heavily black and Hispanic, and in a few, mainly on the West Coast, people from the Far East have concentrated in neighborhoods.

The second great wave of immigrants to the United States began around 1960 and continues to the present. This wave has traveled mainly from the less developed countries of the Western Hemisphere and from Asia. Hispanics have come in such great numbers that they have created "barrios" in many of the nation's largest cities. Foreign blacks mainly have settled in older black ghettos. Within barrios there is a high degree of residential integration between Hispanics of different nationalities. Since most immigrants to the United States quickly learn to drive and purchase cars, ethnic and national cohesion is maintained more through various social institutions and commercial establishments reachable by automobile than through ethnically homogeneous neighborhoods. These institutions include places of worship, ethnic meeting centers, and strip malls where shops and restaurants have opened to cater to ethnic needs.

Today, despite legislation enacted to reduce housing discrimination, most blacks—both those whose ancestors arrived centuries ago and those who arrived recently—continue to live in racially homogeneous neighborhoods. The two central reasons for this homogeneity are the unwillingness of members of other races to live in predominately black neighborhoods and the poverty that prevents blacks from leaving their own neighborhoods. Moreover, many blacks choose to remain in these neighborhoods for cultural reasons. During the past 40 years many middle-class blacks have left the older ghettos to establish more affluent black neighborhoods or to move to white neighborhoods. This has led to a sharp increase in the isolation of low-income black households from affluent black households. Today in Florida's large cities as elsewhere in the nation, poor and affluent blacks are almost as isolated, and in some cases are even more isolated, from each other as the non-Hispanic white poor from the non-Hispanic white wealthy.

Gold Coast Urban Region

Florida's Gold Coast is the state's most populous urban region and also its most racially and ancestrally complex (see table 5.1). The Gold Coast provides an excellent model for examining how population groups distribute themselves within cities. Although the Gold Coast actually includes three U.S. Census "Metropolitan Statistical Areas," they together form a solidly urban area that reaches 10 to 20 miles inland from the Atlantic Coast between Miami-Dade and Palm Beach counties. Thirty-two percent of the state's population lives within it, but so do 41 percent of the state's blacks and 64 percent of its Hispanics. Within the Hispanic category, the Gold Coast has an 87–percent share of the state's Cubans. In fact, of the 21 Latin American nationalities identified in the 2000 census, 16 had at least three-quarters of their Florida population living on the Gold Coast. There were 17 other nationalities—principally African and those from the non-Hispanic Western Hemisphere—with over half their Florida population living there. Whereas the Gold Coast once was nationally famous for its retirees, in 2000 only 23 percent of its population was non-Hispanic and 65 years of age and older. Its share of non-Hispanic whites under 65 in that year was even lower: 21 percent compared to 32 percent in 1960.

Most Hispanics who have come to live on the Gold Coast have chosen Miami-Dade County as their home. Their arrival was accompanied by the departure from the county of many non-Hispanic whites, and few have arrived to replace them. Whereas in 1960, Hispanics held only a 5-percent share of Miami-Dade's population, by 2000 their share had risen to 57 percent. During the same 40-year period—one in which the county's total population rose by 1.3 million—the share of non-Hispanic whites fell from 80 percent to 21 percent. Most non-Hispanic whites who now move to Florida or relocate within it choose to live elsewhere in the state, including the two Gold Coast counties to the north of Miami-Dade County.

The diffusion of both blacks and Hispanics throughout Miami-Dade County since 1970 has been in two different directions. The Hispanics have mainly moved westward, northwestward, and southward from their core area just to the west of Miami's central business district (Fig. 5.1). The most important advance of Miami's black population has been northward, although there has been some expansion from older, relatively small black enclaves in the southern half of the county (Fig. 5.2).

Most of the territorial expansion of blacks and Hispanics has been into areas previously dominated by large majorities of non-Hispanic whites. In most cases, the tracts already had a large population. In the case of the Hispanics but not the blacks, some tracts were situated on the fringe of urban Miami-Dade County and were lightly populated. There were only a few tracts where a previously black majority was replaced by a Hispanic majority. There were no tracts where the opposite was true. The notable exceptions occurred mainly in or near Miami's central business district. Whereas in earlier decades the population of these tracts was heavily black, by 2000 Hispanics had attained at least 40 percent of their total population. The poverty rate in most of these tracts was more than double that of the county.

It is interesting to examine the transition of the populations of two communities in Miami-Dade County since 1960. Hialeah, which in 1960 had a population of 66,972, was in the path of Hispanic diffusion. In 2000 it had grown to 226,411, most of that growth from Hispanic influx. In 1960, almost 100 percent of its population was non-Hispanic white. During the 1970s it surpassed half

Census Year that the Hispanic Population First Reached 40 Percent of the Total Census Tract Population in Miami-Dade County

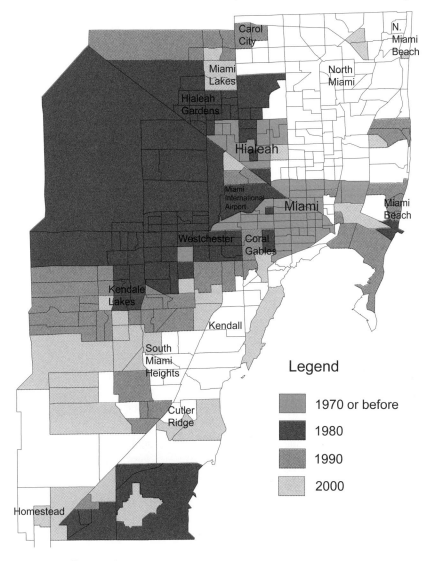

Fig. 5.1. Diffusion of Hispanics in Miami-Dade County.

Census Year that the Black Population First Reached 40 Percent of the Total Census Tract Population in Miami-Dade County

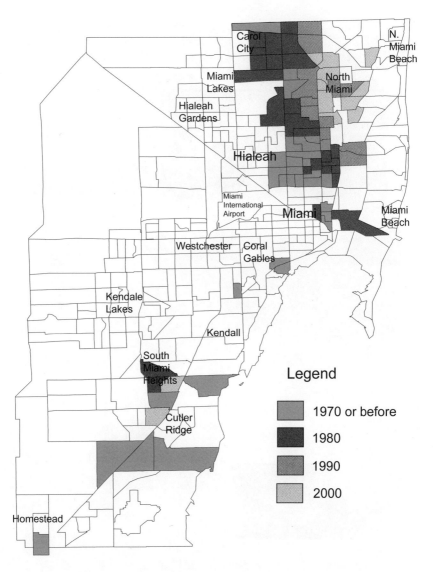

Fig. 5.2. Diffusion of Blacks in Miami-Dade County.

Table 5.1. The share of races and ancestry groups in the Gold Coast urban region compared with their share in the nation's total

Race	Population	Quotient
Non-Hispanic	3,395,977	0.75
Hispanic	**1,785,004**	**2.64**
Non-Hispanic white	2,242,990	0.63
Hispanic white	**1,472,184**	**4.38**
Non-Hispanic black	**898,846**	**1.51**
Hispanic black	**54,654**	**2.94**
Non-Hispanic American Indian	15,183	0.25
Hispanic American Indian	8,119	0.67
Non-Hispanic "other"	**67,112**	**2.11**
Hispanic "other"	242,883	0.81

HISPANIC AMERICAN AND BRAZILIAN

Spanish American	**2,732**	**2.01**
Cuban	**726,898**	**32.63**
Dominican Republican	**50,601**	**3.69**
Puerto Rican	**160,435**	**2.63**
Costa Rican	**7,227**	**5.87**
Guatemalan	**18,846**	**2.82**
Honduran	**33,386**	**8.55**
Mexican	87,645	0.24
Nicaraguan	**74,521**	**23.38**
Panamanian	**8,508**	**5.17**
Salvadorian	**14,856**	**1.26**
Argentinean	**18,928**	**10.46**
Bolivian	**3,403**	**4.51**
Brazilian	**23,731**	**8.08**
Chilean	**10,932**	**8.85**
Colombian	**108,574**	**12.86**
Ecuadorian	**17,181**	**3.68**
Peruvian	35,743	8.52
Uruguayan	3,374	4.36
Venezuelan	**32,236**	**19.63**

OTHER WESTERN HEMISPHERE GROUPS

Bahamian	**14,032**	**28.35**
Barbadian	**2,162**	**2.37**
Belizean	**1,475**	**2.35**
British West Indian	**6,131**	**4.22**
Canadian	**15,246**	**1.76**
French Canadian	22,651	0.68

continued

Table 5.1.—*Continued*

Race	Population	Quotient
Guyanese	**5,206**	**1.92**
Haitian	**185,872**	**19.44**
Jamaican	**121,646**	**9.84**
Trinidadian and Tobagonian	**12,814**	**4.67**
United States, or American	268,711	0.73
U.S. Virgin Islander	**1,824**	**7.31**
EUROPEAN		
Austrian	**16,680**	**2.13**
Basque	1,049	0.44
Belgian	2,509	0.62
British	15,153	0.97
Bulgarian	1,086	0.97
Czechoslovakian (including Slovak)	13,319	0.68
Danish	5,230	0.34
Dutch	20,366	0.44
English	154,431	0.52
Finnish	5,792	0.74
French (except Basque)	51,498	0.59
German	221,918	0.41
Greek	17,572	1.04
Hungarian	**23,747**	**1.46**
Irish	206,394	0.60
Italian	267,123	1.15
Latvian	1,800	0.60
Lithuanian	8,105	1.07
Norwegian	13,557	0.23
Polish	93,995	0.83
Portuguese	12,837	0.78
Romanian	**12,971**	**2.70**
Russian	**102,055**	**2.95**
Scandinavian	1,818	0.33
Scotch-Irish	25,234	0.43
Scotch	30,043	0.53
Spanish or Spaniard	**25,025**	**1.50**
Swedish	18,173	0.42
Ukrainian	10,581	0.89
Welsh	7,637	0.48
Yugoslavian (also Croat, Macedonian, Serbian, Slovene)	6,494	0.47

Race	Population	Quotient
MIDDLE EASTERN AND NORTH AFRICAN		
Egyptian	2,136	0.89
Iranian	3,941	0.69
Israeli	**6,608**	**3.82**
Lebanese	**10,700**	**1.71**
Moroccan	1,370	0.56
Palestinian	**2,108**	**1.74**
Syrian	**2,925**	**1.53**
Turkish	**4,263**	**2.40**
SUB-SAHARAN AFRICAN		
Nigerian	2,536	0.87
South African	**2,017**	**1.53**
Other Asian		
Armenian	2,777	0.46
Asian Indian	29,099	0.96
Chinese (including Taiwanese)	21,663	0.50
Filipino	11,292	0.34
Japanese	3,052	0.21
Korean	4,570	0.24
Pakistani	2,850	1.03
Thai	1,831	0.90
Vietnamese	5,913	0.29
MISCELLANEOUS		
Non-Hispanic white, 65 and over	542,272	1.03

Only groups of 1,000 or more are identified. Quotients represent the percentage of a group in the urban region divided by the group's share in the total U.S. population. Any share 25 percent or higher (1.25) than the U.S. percentage is highlighted.

Hispanic, and it has kept rising until, by 2000, it reached 90 percent, almost all white. North Miami was in the path of black expansion, which began later than the Hispanic. In 1960 it had a population of 28,708, almost 100 percent non-Hispanic white, and many of these were at least 65 years of age. By 2000 its population had risen to 60,036 and its share of non-Hispanic whites had fallen precipitously. Blacks reached one-quarter of the population during the 1980s, and by 2000 had risen to over half (52 percent). By then, the non-Hispanic white population had fallen to 18 percent, but the Hispanic population had risen to 24 percent.

Although the Gold Coast had a modest Hispanic population before the successful Cuban social revolution of 1959, it was only after the revolution that its numbers began to increase rapidly. Today, approximately two million Hispanics live on the Gold Coast, and almost three-quarters of them live in Miami-Dade County. The region has become one of the most attractive in the nation for people from Latin America, particularly those from the Caribbean (table 5.1). Today the county has one of the highest percentages of Hispanics in the nation. As previously mentioned, as the Hispanic population of Miami-Dade County grew, the county became less attractive to other ancestry and racial groups. Also its share of non-Hispanic white retirees has declined precipitously. Whereas as late as 1980 it had a higher share of non-Hispanic white elderly than most metropolitan counties in the nation, today it is decidedly among the more youthful. Although the census does not separate blacks of recent Caribbean origin from African-Americans, there is strong evidence that the latter are abandoning Miami-Dade County for Broward and counties elsewhere in Florida.

Miami-Dade County's loss in the number of non-Hispanic retirees was partially compensated by increases in their numbers within the other two Gold Coast counties. Nonetheless, since 1960, retirees coming to Florida have found the Gold Coast less attractive. In 1960 approximately one-third of the state's non-Hispanic white population 65 years of age and older lived within the region, but by 2000 the share had fallen to 23 percent. The decline in the share of the state's elderly living on the Gold Coast would have been much greater were it not for the continuing enthusiasm of Jewish retirees to move there. As previously mentioned, the U.S. Census no longer identifies people by religion. However, Russians have been used as a surrogate for Jews, and their distribution has been mapped. Many Jews now live in planned unit communities within Broward and Palm Beach counties that have been built specifically to cater to them.

Except for the blacks, and to a lesser degree the Cubans, all the other racial and ancestry groups on the Gold Coast live in census tracts where they are in the minority. Most blacks on the Gold Coast live in tracts that are overwhelmingly black. In 2000, there were 32 Gold Coast tracts that were over 90 percent black. In another 51 tracts, the group held between a 70-percent and a 90-percent share of the total population. Black neighborhoods formed on the Gold Coast early in the twentieth century and are scattered from the southern to the northern part of the region. Their populations have grown dramatically since the 1960s, when the Gold Coast began to receive large numbers of American blacks from elsewhere in Florida as well as other states, namely southern, and those from the Caribbean. Northeastern Miami-Dade County has become particularly attractive to Caribbean blacks. It is within this ghetto that Little Haiti formed.

Many tracts within the Gold Coast are over 90 percent Hispanic. The Cuban ancestry group, however, was the only one whose members made up at least half the total population of a tract. It should be noted that in 2000 there were almost 750,000 Cubans living on the Gold Coast. In two of Miami-Dade County's tracts, located in the heart of Little Havana, Cubans constituted at least 75 percent of the population. In 67 other Miami–Dade County tracts the Cuban share of the population was between 50 and 69 percent. In no Gold Coast tracts did the shares of any other nationality rise above 35 percent. For most, the tract with the highest share was about 20 percent.

Choice of a residence on the Gold Coast, as elsewhere in the United States, is usually based on household income. The importance of household income to a group's geographic distribution is best understood by identifying the Gold Coast tracts that in 1999 had a median per capita income of $30,000 or less and $60,000 or more. In 1999, a median income of $30,000 would have been considered low and one of $60,000 high. Although there were poor households in high-median income tracts and high-income households in low-median income tracts, the majority of households in each tract generally reflected the tract's median income. It follows that if one group has a larger share than another group living in either the poorer or wealthier tracts, the geographical distribution of the two groups in the Gold Coast would differ. Those Hispanic nationalities with the largest shares of households living in the region's poorest tracts were the Hondurans, Nicaraguans, Salvadorans, Cubans, and Dominicans. All had at least 30 percent of their households living in the poorest tracts (table 5.2). The Hispanic nationalities with the lowest share of households living in the poorest tracts were all from South America: Venezuelans, Colombians, Brazilians, and Ecuadorians. All had only between 14 and 18 percent of their households living in the poorest tracts.

Table 5.2. Percent of group living in poor and affluent tracts on the Gold Coast

Race	Poor(%)	Affluent(%)
Total population	24	18
Total non-Hispanics	22	20
Total Hispanics	28	15
Non-Hispanic whites	12	27
Hispanic whites	28	16
Non-Hispanic blacks	45	5
Hispanic blacks	43	8
Non-Hispanic American Indians	24	13
Hispanic American Indians	35	9
Non-Hispanic Asians	13	26
Hispanic Asians	23	20
Non-Hispanic "others"	34	10
Hispanic "others"	30	11
HISPANIC		
Total Hispanic	28	15
Argentinean	22	20
Brazilian	18	18
Chilean	19	21
Colombian	16	22
Costa Rican	24	15
Cuban	30	14
Dominican Republican	30	13
Ecuadorian	18	22
Guatemalan	31	7
Honduran	50	6
Mexican	29	9
Nicaraguan	43	10
Panamanian	21	20
Peruvian	19	20
Puerto Rican	24	15
Salvadorian	31	11
Venezuelan	14	29
OTHER WESTERN HEMISPHERE GROUPS		
Canadian	16	26
French Canadian	17	20
Guyanese	21	16
United States or American	19	22
Total West Indian	36	7
Bahamian	44	6
British West Indies	33	7
Haitian	43	3
Jamaican	28	11
Trinidadian or Tobagonian	20	15

EUROPEAN

Austrian	16	27
British	11	29
Czechoslovakian (including Slovak)	12	25
Danish	10	27
Dutch	10	27
English	9	29
Finnish	16	18
French (except Basque)	11	25
German	9	27
Greek	10	30
Hungarian	14	26
Irish	9	26
Italian	10	28
Lithuanian	13	26
Norwegian	9	30
Polish	13	28
Portuguese	14	22
Romanian	23	20
Russian	13	33
Scotch-Irish	8	27
Scotch	9	29
Spanish	19	26
Swedish	9	26
Swiss	7	34
Ukrainian	16	24
Welsh	10	25
Yugoslavian (also Croat, Macedonia, Serbian, Slovene)	11	25

MIDDLE EASTERN AND NORTH AFRICAN

Total Arab	11	29
Lebanese	11	33
Iranian	8	45
Israeli	7	34
Turkish	18	24

SUB-SAHARAN AFRICAN

Total sub-Saharan African	37	11

OTHER ASIAN

Asian Indian	13	25
Chinese (including Taiwanese)	11	30
Filipino	14	27
Japanese	12	31
Korean	10	36
Pakistani	13	21
Vietnamese	11	22

Note: Only those groups with 3,000 or more residents are identified Poor households are those with a median income in 1999 of $30,000 or less. Affluent households are those with a median income in 1999 of $60,000 or more.

Among different non-Hispanic black groups, there also were differences in the share of households living in the poorer tracts. Although most blacks, regardless of their income, continue to live in predominately black neighborhoods, a higher percentage of some groups live in more affluent tracts than others. On the Gold Coast, for example, only 28 percent of Jamaicans lived within the poorest tracts compared to 43 percent of the Haitians and 44 percent of the Bahamians. The differences between the shares of European and Asian ancestry groups who lived in the Gold Coast's poorest tracts were small: most were between 10 and 15 percent.

Certain parts of Miami-Dade County have acquired names that suggest a homogeneous population like that of Little Havana. "Little Managua" is situated in suburban Sweetwater, for example. Part of North Miami Beach has become associated with Argentines, and many Mexicans, and to a lesser extent Guatemalans and Salvadorians, live in the southern part of Miami-Dade County, where they are the main labor source for area farms. Yet the percentage of people of these nationalities in the total population of the tracts where they are concentrated is often quite small. For example, in the census tract that Nicaraguans would consider being the heart of Little Managua, they comprised only 20 percent of the total population. The tract with the highest percentage of Mexicans (35 percent) was near Homestead, in the southern part of Miami-Dade County. The share of Puerto Ricans in the Gold Coast tract where they were most heavily represented in the population was only 18 percent.

The distribution of nine Gold Coast groups has been cartographically represented in the atlas. They reveal distinct settlement patterns. Blacks are by far the most spatially concentrated, although there are black neighborhoods in all three of the region's counties. The Haitians, the vast majority of whom are black, have settled in most of the older black neighborhoods of the Gold Coast, particularly those of northeastern Miami-Dade County. Cubans remain heavily concentrated in Miami-Dade County as do Nicaraguans. Mexicans, Puerto Ricans, and Venezuelans are far less concentrated. In the case of the Mexicans, many have been attracted to the region's agricultural areas. The result of the non-Hispanic white retiree exodus from Miami-Dade County is clearly evident, as is that of the Jews, who here are represented by people of Russian ancestry.

Tampa Bay Urban Region

Tampa Bay, Florida's second largest urban region, here includes the counties in which Tampa and St. Petersburg are situated (Hillsborough and Pinellas),

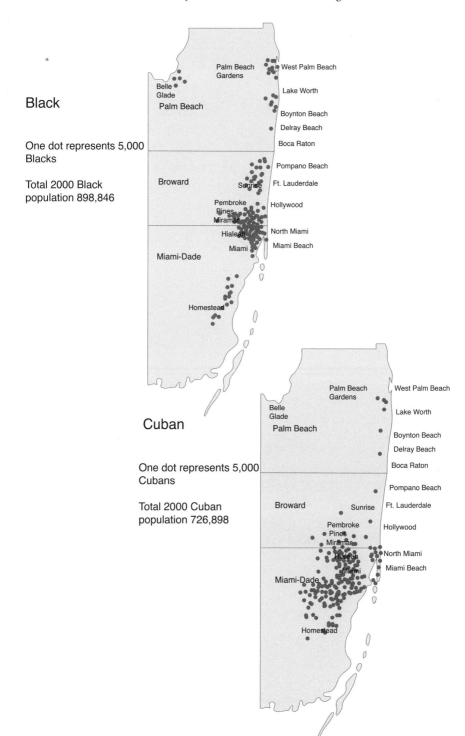

Black

One dot represents 5,000 Blacks

Total 2000 Black population 898,846

Cuban

One dot represents 5,000 Cubans

Total 2000 Cuban population 726,898

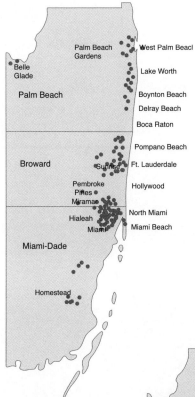

Haitian

One dot represents 1,000
Haitians

Total 2000 Haitian
population 185,872

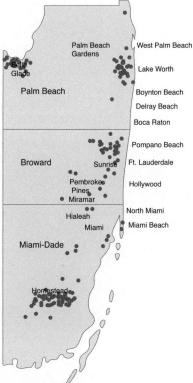

Mexican

One dot represents 500
Mexicans

Total 2000 Mexican
population 87,645

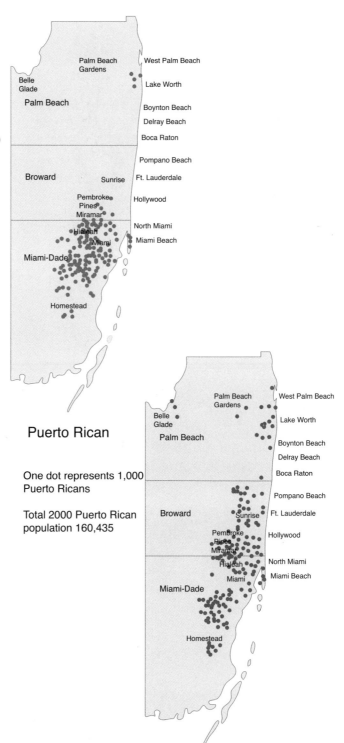

Nicaraguan

One dot represents 250
Nicaraguans

Total 2000 Nicaraguan
population 74,521

Palm Beach
Gardens
West Palm Beach
Belle
Glade
Lake Worth
Palm Beach
Boynton Beach
Delray Beach
Boca Raton
Pompano Beach
Broward
Sunrise
Ft. Lauderdale
Pembroke
Pines
Miramar
Hollywood
North Miami
Hialeah
Miami
Miami Beach
Miami-Dade
Homestead

Puerto Rican

One dot represents 1,000
Puerto Ricans

Total 2000 Puerto Rican
population 160,435

Palm Beach
Gardens
West Palm Beach
Belle
Glade
Lake Worth
Palm Beach
Boynton Beach
Delray Beach
Boca Raton
Pompano Beach
Broward
Sunrise
Ft. Lauderdale
Pembroke
Pines
Miramar
Hollywood
Hialeah
North Miami
Miami
Miami Beach
Miami-Dade
Homestead

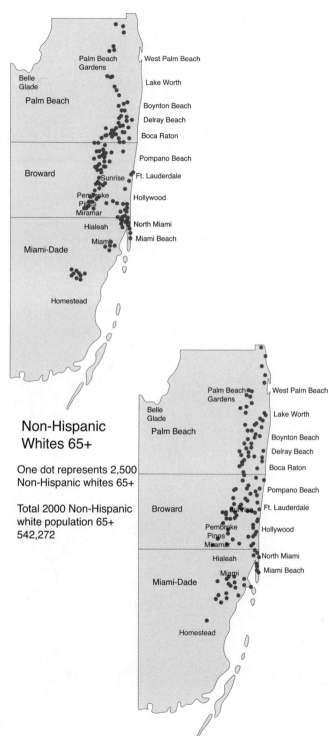

Russian

One dot represents 750 Russians

Total 2000 Russian population 102,055

Non-Hispanic Whites 65+

One dot represents 2,500 Non-Hispanic whites 65+

Total 2000 Non-Hispanic white population 65+ 542,272

Venezuelan

One dot represents 250 Venezuelans

Total 2000 Venezuelan population 32,236

as well as the two counties immediately to the north of St. Petersburg (Pasco and Hernando). With the exception of Key West, Tampa Bay developed ethnic neighborhoods earlier than any other Florida city. In fact, the failure of Key West to rebuild its cigar industry after a series of fires and labor disputes during the 1880s brought about the growth of the cigar industry in Tampa and to a lesser extent in Jacksonville. Thousands of Cubans and Spaniards left Key West to work in Tampa's cigar factories, and they were joined by a large number of Italian immigrants. The majority of workers lived in Tampa's Ybor City, where most of the factories were located. At the beginning of the twentieth century, Greeks arrived from the Florida Keys to live in Pinellas County where they established an ethnic neighborhood in Tarpon Springs.

The Tampa Bay region has not had as great a part as the Gold Coast and Orlando urban regions in the nation's recent wave of international immigration that began during the 1960s. Nonetheless, its Hispanic community is large as is its population from the non-Hispanic Caribbean (table 5.3). Although its share of the state's non-Hispanic elderly has been in decline for the past 30 years, the Tampa Bay region still has a larger share of this group than the other three urban regions here examined. While the share of the non-Hispanic white aged in the total population of the other three urban regions is close to that of their share in the nation's total population, the share of this group in the total population of the Tampa Bay region remains well above that of the nation. The share of non-Hispanic blacks within its population is the lowest of the four urban regions.

Blacks are the only highly concentrated population within the urban region. At the time of the 2000 census, the share of blacks was at least half the total population in 47 tracts. There was, however, one tract in the agricultural area of eastern Hillsborough County where half the population was Mexican. Although Tarpon Springs' Greek population regularly receives national attention, the Greek share of its total population was only 20 percent—even within the tract where the town is located.

Following the end of the Vietnam War, many Vietnamese fled the country and were joined by smaller numbers from Laos and Cambodia. By 2000, there were living in the Tampa Bay region 9,318 Vietnamese, 1,765 Laotians, and 682 Cambodians. Of Florida's four largest urban areas, Tampa Bay has by far the largest number of Vietnamese and Laotians and the second largest number of Cambodians. A large concentration of Vietnamese and Laotians developed in southern Pinellas County. Here the Martyrs Pastoral Mission, a Catholic church, has contributed greatly to their assimilation. A second concentration, consisting mainly of Vietnamese, has developed on the eastern side of Tampa. Thais, who in 2000 numbered 1,271 in the Tampa area, are distributed in a manner similar to the Vietnamese.

The non-Hispanic white elderly also have demonstrated a tendency to concentrate. In 2000 there were 18 census tracts in the Tampa Bay area where retirees constituted at least half the total population. Most were in Pinellas County, where retirees long have had a major presence. Over the past 40 years, however, the group has diffused northward along the Gulf Coast into Pasco and Hernando counties and even beyond. Here a number of planned unit developments have been built specifically for them.

The nine Tampa Bay groups whose distributions have been mapped confirm what already has been noted: the concentration of Greeks and Vietnamese is obvious as is the concentration of Cubans. The latter, many descended from Cubans who arrived in the early part of the last century to work in the cigar factories, continue to concentrate in or near Ybor City. Ybor City, however, has developed into one of the region's most important amusement areas

Table 5.3. The share of races and ancestry groups in the Tampa Bay urban region compared with their share in the nation's total

Race	Total	Quotient
Non-Hispanic	2,181,428	1.03
Hispanic	264,235	0.83
Non-Hispanic white	1,847,789	1.10
Hispanic white	176,776	1.11
Non-Hispanic black	235,500	0.83
Hispanic black	10,033	1.14
Non-Hispanic American Indian	16,334	0.56
Hispanic American Indian	2,931	0.51
Non-Hispanic "other"	13,537	0.90
Hispanic "other"	72,377	0.51

HISPANIC AMERICAN AND BRAZILIAN

Spanish American	**1,329**	**2.07**
Cuban	**41,602**	**3.96**
Dominican Republican	4,992	0.77
Puerto Rican	**75,621**	**2.62**
Costa Rican	**1,045**	**1.80**
Guatemalan	1,203	0.38
Honduran	2,213	1.20
Mexican	53,732	0.31
Nicaraguan	913	0.61
Panamanian	**1,653**	**2.13**
Salvadorian	1,194	0.22
Argentinean	786	0.92
Brazilian	1,593	1.15
Colombian	**7,738**	**1.94**
Ecuadorian	1,740	0.79
Peruvian	2,245	1.13
Venezuelan	**2,190**	**2.83**

OTHER WESTERN HEMISPHERE GROUPS

Bahamian	**510**	**2.18**
Barbadian	508	1.19
British West Indian	802	1.19
Canadian	**8,903**	**2.17**
French Canadian	**20,649**	**1.31**
Guyanese	1,303	1.01
Haitian	3,773	0.84
Jamaican	**8,160**	**1.40**

continued

Table 5.3.—*Continued*

Race	Total	Quotient
Trinidadian and Tobagonian	**1,683**	**1.29**
United States or American	178,814	1.02
EUROPEAN		
Albanian	**1,510**	**1.74**
Austrian	**4,689**	**1.27**
Belgian	1,723	0.90
British	**11,413**	**1.55**
Bulgarian	**780**	**1.97**
Czechoslovakian (including Slovaks)	**13,748**	**1.50**
Danish	5,234	0.72
Dutch	22,812	1.05
English	**188,910**	**1.34**
Finnish	2,929	0.79
French (except Basque)	50,927	1.23
German	255,445	1.00
Greek	**19,566**	**2.45**
Hungarian	**11,879**	**1.55**
Irish	200,440	1.23
Italian	**166,658**	**1.52**
Latvian	**797**	**1.40**
Lithuanian	**5,766**	**1.61**
Norwegian	16,295	0.59
Polish	58,572	1.10
Portuguese	6,329	0.82
Romanian	**1,865**	**0.82**
Russian	**13,996**	**0.86**
Scandinavian	1,807	0.69
Scotch-Irish	33,883	1.22
Scotch	**37,142**	**1.40**
Spanish or Spaniard	**13,197**	**2.02**
Swedish	19,561	0.95
Swiss	4,065	0.89
Ukrainian	5,695	1.01
Welsh	**9,585**	**1.28**
Yugoslavian (also Croat, Macedonian, Serbian, Slovene)	7,286	1.11
MIDDLE EAST AND NORTH AFRICA		
Egyptian	1,042	0.92
Iranian	1,093	0.41
Lebanese	3,440	1.17
Palestinian	**896**	**1.56**

Race	Total	Quotient
Syrian	**1,336**	**1.47**
Turkish	1,047	1.24
SUB SAHARAN AFRICA		
Nigerian	520	0.38
South African	**595**	**1.67**
OTHER ASIAN		
Armenian	1,305	0.46
Asian Indian	10,854	0.76
Cambodian	**682**	**4.46**
Chinese (including Taiwanese)	5,630	0.27
Filipino	7,499	0.48
Japanese	1,572	0.23
Korean	3,609	0.40
Laotian	1,765	1.13
Thai	1,271	0.33
Vietnamese	**9,318**	**1.33**
MISCELLANEOUS		
Australian	594	1.12
Non Hispanic whites 65 or Older	**415,048**	**1.67**

Only groups of 500 or more are identified. Quotients represent the percentage of a group in the urban region divided by the group's share in the total U.S. population. Any share 25 or more percent higher (1.25) than the U.S. percentage is highlighted.

and now lies on the periphery of the Cuban concentration. The strong attraction of Florida's waterfronts to non-Hispanic white retirees can be seen from their high concentration along the Gulf of Mexico from St. Petersburg north to beyond Spring Hill in Hernando County.

Orlando Urban Region

The Orlando area is smaller in total population than both the Gold Coast and the Tampa Bay regions. In racial and ancestry diversity, however, it is far more complex than the Tampa Bay region, but far less so than the Gold Coast. Until the 1960s, compared with the other three urban regions of Florida, the population of Orlando was small. Floridians tended to regard Orlando as a "cow town," since most of the land immediately to the south was devoted to cattle ranching. During the 1960s, Disney World opened; it became and remains the most well-attended theme park in the world. The success of Disney World motivated the construction of several other large theme parks in the Orlando urban region as well as a number of smaller ones. Greater Orlando has become one of the most important tourist destinations in the world, and each year it is visited by tens of millions of visitors, many from overseas. Tourism—today the city's major source of income—has created hundreds of thousands of low-wage service jobs. Although most of these jobs have been filled by people from elsewhere in the United States, many have come from other nations, particularly from those in the Western Hemisphere, seeking employment (table 5.4).

The Orlando area also has become attractive to American blacks, both native and foreign-born. Although it does not yet rival Atlanta as a destination for American blacks, it is one of four Southern cities most favored by them. The other two are Charlotte and Dallas. As in Florida's other urban regions, in the Orlando area, blacks comprise the only racial or ancestry group that is truly spatially concentrated. In 29 tracts, blacks constituted at least half of the total population, and in eight tracts, they accounted for at least 90 percent of the population. These tracts are shared by blacks descended from slaves who arrived in Florida many generations ago, as well as by blacks from other nations, particularly the Caribbean islands.

Puerto Ricans have become Orlando's largest Hispanic group, and today there are about as many Puerto Ricans living there as on the Gold Coast. Many come directly from Puerto Rico, but even more are arriving from elsewhere in the United States, including large numbers who have chosen it as a place of retirement. In 2000, there were two tracts in northern Osceola County,

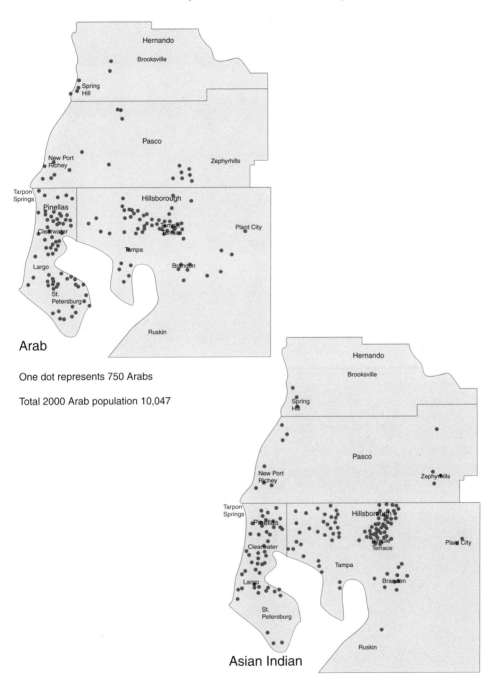

Arab

One dot represents 750 Arabs

Total 2000 Arab population 10,047

Asian Indian

One dot represents 100 Asian Indians

Total 2000 Asian Indian population 10,854

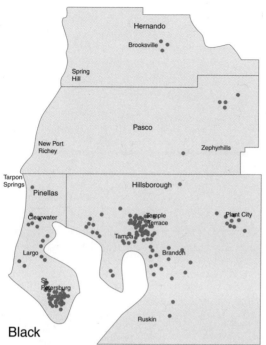

Black

One dot represents 1,500 Blacks

Total 2000 Black population 235,500

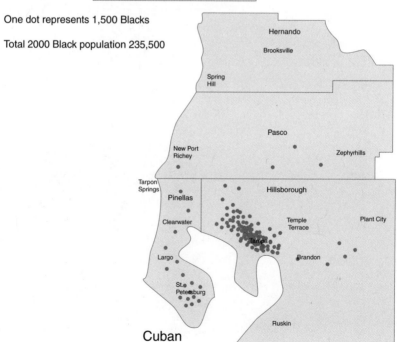

Cuban

One dot represents 250 Cubans

Total 2000 Cuban population 41,602

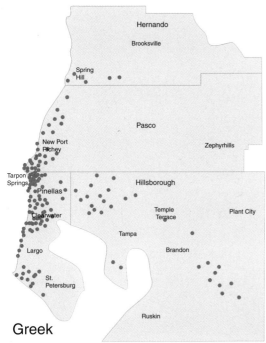

Greek

One dot represents 100 Greeks

Total 2000 Greek population 19,566

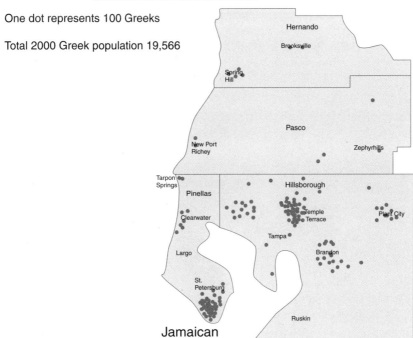

Jamaican

One dot represents 50 Jamaicans

Total 2000 Jamaican population 8,160

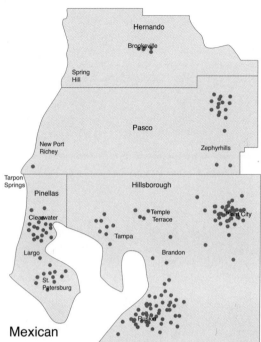

Mexican

One dot represents 400 Mexicans

Total 2000 Mexican population 53,732

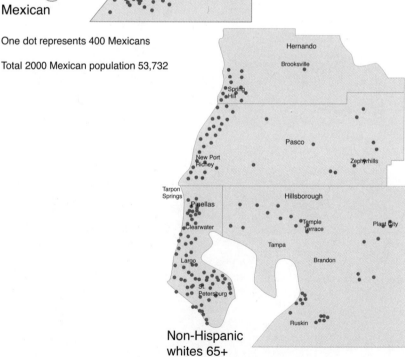

Non-Hispanic whites 65+

One dot represents 3,000 Non-Hispanic whites 65+

Total 2000 Non-Hispanic white population 415,048

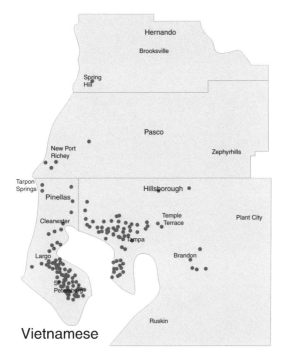

Vietnamese

One dot represents 50 Vietnamese

Total 2000 Vietnamese population 9,318

south of Orange County (Orlando), where Puerto Ricans were very heavily represented in the population. One is 40 percent Puerto Rican and the other 49 percent. The town of Kissimmee, which has become well known as a destination for Puerto Ricans, is on the southern edge of this concentration.

Except for the Mexicans, most other Hispanics in the Orlando urban region have not concentrated to the degree that Puerto Ricans have. The majority, however, do live in its more densely populated neighborhoods. On the western side of the urban region, agriculture and food processing are important. These activities have drawn many Mexicans. This same area has attracted many non-Hispanic white retirees, among them a considerable number of Canadians. In and around Leesburg in 2000 there were six tracts in which non-Hispanic white retirees held at least a 40–percent share of the total population.

The Orlando urban region has the second largest Vietnamese population of the four urban regions identified in this study, but compared to the Tampa

Table 5.4. The share of races and ancestry groups in the Orlando urban region compared with their share in the nation's total

Race	Population	Quotient
Non-Hispanic	1,404,440	0.95
Hispanic	**290,202**	**1.31**
Non-Hispanic white	1,089,606	0.94
Hispanic white	**177,369**	**1.61**
Non-Hispanic black	216,779	1.12
Hispanic black	**12,811**	**2.11**
Non-Hispanic American Indian	10,127	0.50
Hispanic American Indian	2,684	0.68
Non-Hispanic "other"	**17,539**	**1.69**
Hispanic "other"	95,082	0.97
HISPANIC AMERICAN AND BRAZILIAN		
Spanish American	547	1.23
Cuban	**18,797**	**2.58**
Dominican Republican	**9,996**	**2.23**
Puerto Rican	**139,898**	**7.00**
Costa Rican	**1,060**	**2.63**
Guatemalan	1,430	0.65
Honduran	**1,772**	**1.39**
Mexican	32,664	0.27
Nicaraguan	1,285	1.23
Panamanian	**1,765**	**3.28**
Salvadorian	1,727	0.45
blackinean	**1,413**	**2.39**
Bolivian	**310**	**1.26**
Brazilian	**4,328**	**4.51**
Chilean	**719**	**1.78**
Colombian	**12,100**	**4.40**
Ecuadorian	**2,705**	**1.77**
Peruvian	**2,861**	**2.08**
Venezuelan	**3,648**	**6.79**
OTHER WESTERN HEMISPHERE GROUPS		
Bahamian	**785**	**4.85**
Barbadian	**914**	**3.12**
British West Indian	**1,321**	**2.84**
Canadian	**4,201**	**1.49**
French Canadian	11,915	1.09
Guyanese	**2,462**	**2.78**
Haitian	**18,182**	**5.83**
Jamaican	**14,309**	**3.54**

Race	Population	Quotient
Trinidadian and Tobagonian	**2,809**	**3.13**
United States or American	127,418	1.05
U.S. Virgin Islander	**696**	**8.71**
EUROPEAN		
Albanian	462	0.77
Austrian	2,481	0.97
Belgian	1,007	0.76
British	**7,820**	**1.53**
Bulgarian	**376**	**1.38**
Czechoslovakian (including Slovak)	6,988	0.97
Danish	3,435	0.68
Dutch	13,742	0.92
English	116,908	1.20
Finnish	1,460	0.57
French (except Basque)	29,087	1.02
German	147,597	0.83
Greek	4,703	0.85
Hungarian	5,794	1.09
Icelander	**315**	**1.77**
Irish	113,255	1.00
Italian	80,898	1.07
Lithuanian	2,103	0.85
Norwegian	9,476	0.50
Polish	28,819	0.78
Portuguese	3,944	0.73
Romanian	1,137	0.72
Russian	8,879	0.79
Scandinavian	1,171	0.65
Scotch-Irish	20,433	1.06
Scotch	22,561	1.22
Spanish or Spaniard	4,407	0.96
Swedish	10,543	0.74
Swiss	2,304	0.73
Ukrainian	2,700	0.69
Welsh	5,904	1.14
Yugoslavian (also Croat, Macedonian, Serbian, Slovene)	3,739	0.82
MIDDLE EASTERN AND NORTH AFRICAN		
Cape Verde Islander	422	0.72
Egyptian	**1,166**	**1.48**
Iranian	1,333	0.71

continued

Table 5.4.—*Continued*

Race	Population	Quotient
Israeli	387	0.69
Jordanian	**411**	**1.86**
Lebanese	**2,582**	**1.26**
Moroccan	**927**	**4.75**
Palestinian	**976**	**2.46**
Syrian	677	1.08
Turkish	509	0.87
SUB-SAHARAN AFRICAN		
Ethiopian	301	0.60
Nigerian	468	0.49
South African	**441**	**1.68**
OTHER ASIAN		
Armenian	723	0.36
Asian Indian	**12,952**	**1.31**
Chinese (including Taiwanese)	6,779	0.47
Filipino	7,630	0.70
Japanese	1,676	0.36
Korean	3,338	0.53
Laotian	**422**	**2.48**
Pakistani	**1,161**	**1.29**
Thai	691	1.04
Vietnamese	7,621	1.16
MISCELLANEOUS		
Australian	401	1.12
Non-Hispanic white, 65 and over	149,227	0.97

Note: Only groups of 300 or more identified. Quotients represent the percentage of a group in the urban region divided by the group's share in the total U.S. population. Any share 25 or more percent higher (1.25) than the U.S. percentage is highlighted.

Bay region it has relatively few Cambodians and Laotians. On arrival, many Vietnamese settled near downtown Orlando. Here they rehabilitated an older building to create the Long Van Buddhist Temple, which continues to play a major role in the lives of the urban area's Vietnamese. As they established themselves in the Orlando area and became more affluent, the Vietnamese began to move to the eastern side of the region. As a consequence, land was acquired between Winter Park and Azalea Park for the construction of a much larger temple that flourishes today. The temple is not only a place of worship, but a major Vietnamese social center that provides a variety of social and cultural services.

People from South Asia, particularly Asian Indians, have found the Orlando urban region attractive. In 2000, the urban area held 12,952 Asian Indians, 8,243 Bangladeshis, 757 Sri Lankans, and 462 Pakistanis. The share of all four of these groups is far higher within the total population of the urban region than their share within that of the nation. Moreover, all four live quite well integrated with each other, despite the hostilities that defined relations in their mother countries. They have become well dispersed along the periphery of the city of Orlando and its suburbs. Given the large size of the Asian Indian population, the urban area supports several Hindu religious institutions, as well as the Hindu University of America. The latter, founded in 2001 on land a few miles south of the University of Central Florida, now has a permanent faculty, a small but growing enrollment, and an expanding curriculum.

During the past 25 years, Orlando has experienced rapid growth in its Muslim community. As the community grew, religious and cultural institutions formed to meet members' needs. Most Muslims have located on the east side of the city of Orlando, particularly in and around Azalea Park and Winter Park. In 2005, there were seven Muslim places of worship in the Orlando urban region, along with a large school that provides both religious and secular education. Although Muslims are widely dispersed throughout the city, they are disproportionately represented on the east side. The share of Moroccans and Palestinians in Orlando's total population is especially high compared to their national share. It should be noted that among Orlando's Palestinians, as among other Orlando groups tracing their ancestry to predominately Muslim countries, there may be both Christians and Jews. Most, however, are Muslims.

The nine Orlando groups chosen for cartographic representation—with the exception of the blacks and the non-Hispanic white retirees—show a high degree of similarity in their distributions. Even the black concentration is weakening as many well-educated blacks from elsewhere in the nation and abroad have been arriving and obtaining jobs that permit them a wider choice of residence. Retirees who chose Orlando as their destination have increasingly been attracted to the Leesburg area of Lake County where a number of planned unit developments have been built to cater to them.

Jacksonville Urban Region

Jacksonville, the first city in Florida to reach 50,000 inhabitants, remained the state's largest city during the early twentieth century. In the 1930s, Miami overtook it in population. Today, Jacksonville has the smallest population of the four urban regions here examined. Although Jacksonville continues to be important in manufacturing and finance and has a larger military function than the other three, it has not been a major beneficiary of the great international migration to Florida that began in the 1960s (table 5.5). Consequently, although its population has grown, compared to the other regions there has been little change in its ancestry and racial composition during the twentieth century.

Jacksonville's share of blacks within its total population is larger than the shares of the other three Florida urban regions. As elsewhere in Florida, the

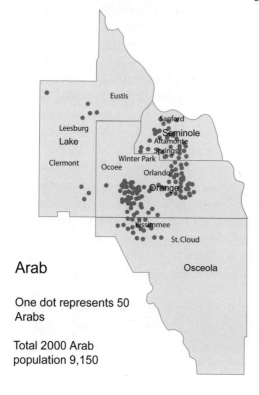

Arab

One dot represents 50
Arabs

Total 2000 Arab
population 9,150

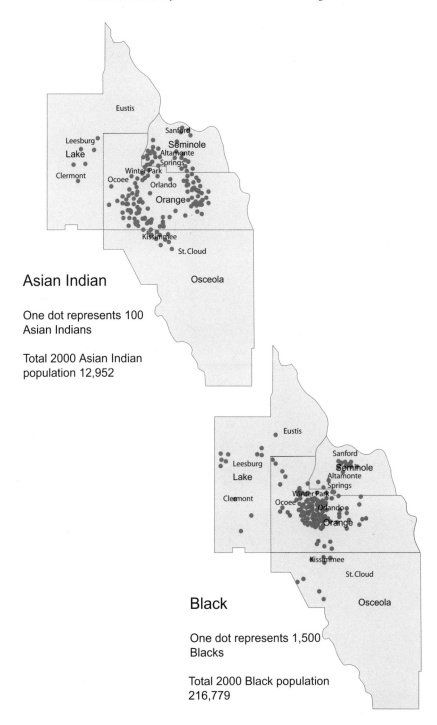

Asian Indian

One dot represents 100
Asian Indians

Total 2000 Asian Indian
population 12,952

Black

One dot represents 1,500
Blacks

Total 2000 Black population
216,779

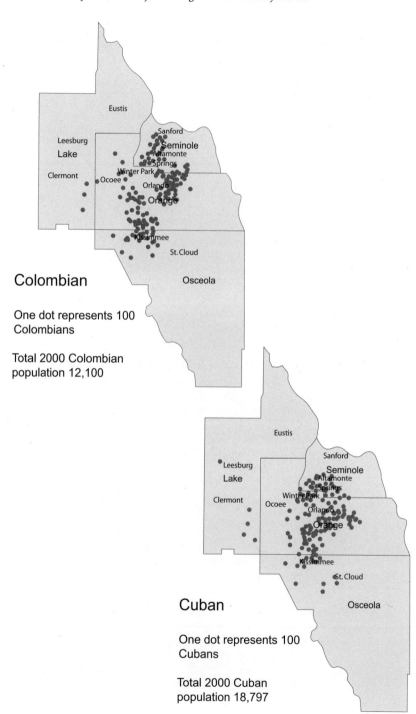

Colombian

One dot represents 100
Colombians

Total 2000 Colombian
population 12,100

Cuban

One dot represents 100
Cubans

Total 2000 Cuban
population 18,797

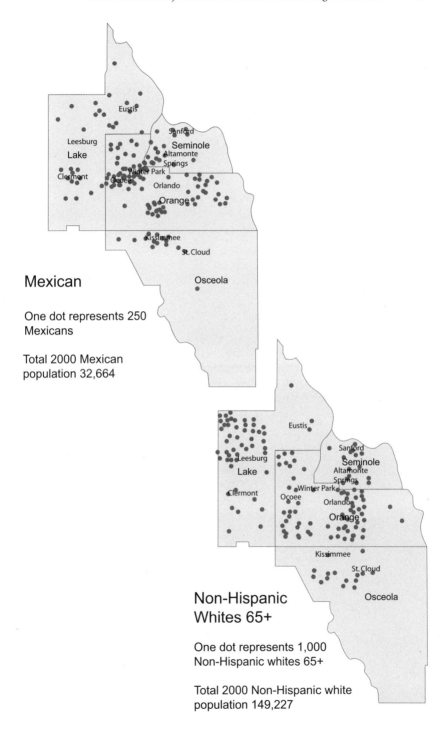

Mexican

One dot represents 250
Mexicans

Total 2000 Mexican
population 32,664

Non-Hispanic
Whites 65+

One dot represents 1,000
Non-Hispanic whites 65+

Total 2000 Non-Hispanic white
population 149,227

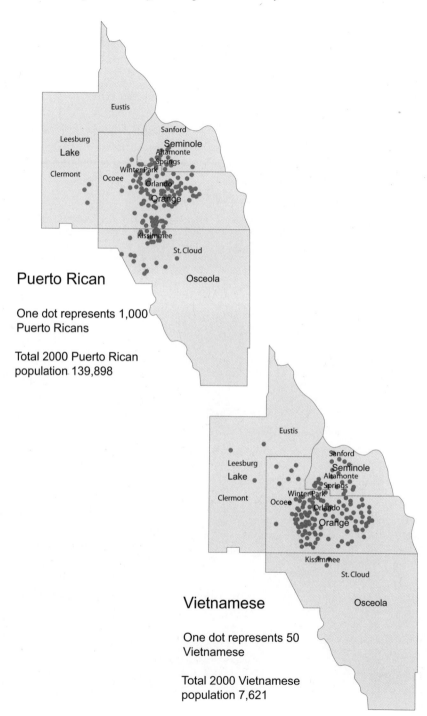

Puerto Rican

One dot represents 1,000
Puerto Ricans

Total 2000 Puerto Rican
population 139,898

Vietnamese

One dot represents 50
Vietnamese

Total 2000 Vietnamese
population 7,621

black population of Jacksonville is highly concentrated. In 19 tracts, its share of the total population was at least 90 percent in 2000. Most of Jacksonville's blacks live near the city's center or to its northwest.

Jacksonville's best-known ethnic minorities are its Middle Easterners, primarily Lebanese, Palestinians, and Syrians. People from this part of the world began to settle in the city in the 1890s. Most became small-scale merchants. In 1920, slightly more than half the city's fruit stands were owned either by Greeks, Lebanese, or Syrians. In the same year, Jews owned approximately half the clothing stores and Chinese over three-quarters of the laundries. Most of these and other foreign immigrants lived at or near their businesses, and no ethnic neighborhoods formed. Although neither Greeks, nor Jews, nor Chinese are particularly well represented in the Jacksonville urban region today, Middle Easterners are. Originally, Middle Easterners who came to Jacksonville were Christian, but today they are mainly Muslim. Their community is well served by an Islamic Center, by several places of worship, and by a school that offers religious as well as secular instruction to children from kindergarten through 12th grade.

Jacksonville is the home of several large U.S. Navy installations. Because so many Filipinos are Navy personnel or are employed as civilians in naval service, that group's share of the Jacksonville urban region's population is much higher than the other three regions' and almost double that of the nation. During the civil war in Yugoslavia, the Jacksonville community made an effort to resettle some its refugees, and today the share of Yugoslavians within its total population, though numerically small, is larger than that of the other three urban regions here examined.

Indicating deep national roots among many of the non-Hispanic whites living in the Jacksonville urban region, a much larger share of its population claimed "United States" ancestry compared to like populations in the other three urban regions. Similarly, compared to the other three urban regions, Jacksonville's also had a larger share of people who claim Scotch-Irish ancestry.

Among the nine population groups for which maps have been drawn, three have been chosen for discussion: Yugoslavians, Arabs, and non-Hispanic white retirees. At the time of the 2000 census, over half (57 percent) of the urban region's Yugoslavians, then numbering over 3,000, were living in five tracts in southern Duval County. Most of these tracts were contiguous with each other, and all but one had a median family income well below that of the urban region's average. Most of the region's Yugoslavians were refugees

Table 5.5. The share of races and ancestry groups in the Jacksonville urban region compared with their share in the nation's total

Race	Population	Quotient
Non-Hispanic	1,075,994	1.10
Hispanic	45,844	0.31
Non-Hispanic white	788,587	1.02
Hispanic white	26,760	0.37
Non-Hispanic black	**234,046**	**1.75**
Hispanic black	3,511	0.87
Non-Hispanic American Indian	8,039	0.60
Hispanic American Indian	715	0.27
Non-Hispanic "other"	6,118	0.89
Hispanic "other"	13,793	0.21
HISPANIC AMERICAN AND BRAZILIAN		
Cuban	4,150	0.86
Dominican Republican	805	0.27
Puerto Rican	14,894	1.13
Costa Rican	328	1.23
Guatemalan	259	0.18
Honduran	332	0.39
Mexican	8,592	0.11
Nicaraguan	316	0.46
Panamanian	**657**	**1.84**
Salvadorian	257	0.10
Colombian	1,227	0.67
Ecuadorian	293	0.29
Peruvian	436	0.48
Venezuelan	281	0.79
OTHER WESTERN HEMISPHERE GROUPS		
British West Indian	5,449	0.81
Canadian	1,908	1.02
French Canadian	5,826	0.81
Guyanese	314	0.54
Haitian	1,148	0.56
Jamaican	2,251	0.84
Trinidadian and Tobagonian	377	0.63
United States or American	**113,838**	**1.42**
EUROPEAN		
Albanian	**863**	**2.12**
Austrian	1,184	0.70
Belgian	634	0.72

Race	Population	Quotient
British	**4,572**	**1.35**
Czechoslovakian (including Slovak)	2,883	0.69
Danish	1,791	0.54
Dutch	7,911	0.80
English	**82,703**	**1.28**
Finnish	1,024	0.61
French (except Basque)	17,980	0.95
German	82,152	0.70
Greek	3,301	0.90
Hungarian	2,797	0.80
Irish	76,442	1.02
Italian	36,231	0.72
Lithuanian	1,318	0.80
Norwegian	6,193	0.49
Polish	13,321	0.54
Portuguese	1,757	0.49
Romanian	761	0.73
Russian	4,143	0.55
Scandinavian	756	0.63
Scotch-Irish	**17,502**	**1.37**
Scotch	**16,236**	**1.33**
Spanish or Spaniard	2,027	0.64
Swedish	5,172	0.55
Swiss	1,198	0.57
Ukrainian	1,704	0.66
Welsh	3,482	1.01
Yugoslavian (also Croat, Macedonian, Serbian, Slovene)	**3,864**	**1.28**
Middle Eastern and North African		
Egyptian	251	0.48
Iranian	457	0.37
Lebanese	**1,750**	**1.29**
Palestinian	**793**	**3.02**
Syrian	**1,296**	**3.13**
Turkish	423	1.10
Sub-Saharan African		
Nigerian	272	0.43
South African	**255**	**1.53**
Other Asian		
Armenian	464	0.35

continued

Table 5.5.—*Continued*

Race	Population	Quotient
Asian Indian	3,311	0.52
Cambodian	**941**	**1.31**
Chinese (including Taiwanese)	1,841	0.21
Filipino	**12,178**	**1.72**
Japanese	767	0.25
Korean	1,386	0.33
Thai	267	0.61
Vietnamese	2,592	0.60
MISCELLANEOUS		
Non-Hispanic white, 65 and over	99,210	0.88

Note: Only groups of 250 or more are identified. Quotients represent the percentage of a group in the urban region divided by the group's share in the total U.S. population. Any share 25 or more percent higher (1.25) than the U.S. percentage is highlighted.

from the civil war who had been invited to resettle there. The Arabs also have become highly concentrated in approximately the same part of the city. In 2000, almost a quarter of the urban region's Arabs were living in seven, mostly contiguous, tracts. These tracts were far more affluent than those occupied by the Yugoslavians. All but one had a median household income over the median for the region, and in one the median income was almost double that of the region. Jacksonville has never been a magnet for non-Hispanic retirees. Recently, however, developers have begun to build communities specifically designed to appeal to them. By 2000, the share of non-Hispanic white retirees within the total population had risen to over 20 percent in several tracts along the coast. Ponte Vedra Beach is probably the region's best-known community with a large share of retired residents.

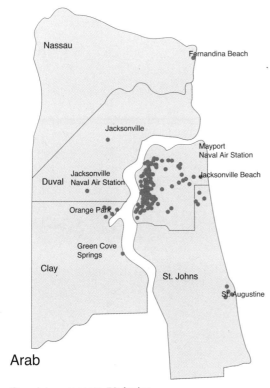

Arab

One dot represents 50 Arabs

Total 2000 Arab population 6,098

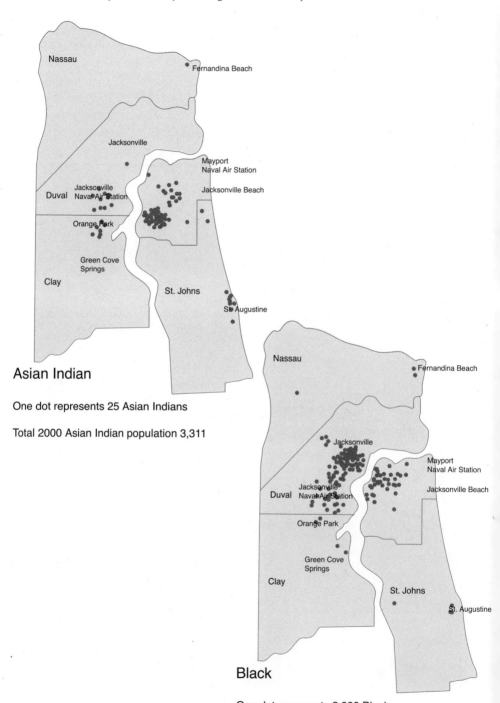

Asian Indian

One dot represents 25 Asian Indians

Total 2000 Asian Indian population 3,311

Black

One dot represents 2,000 Blacks

Total 2000 Black population 234,046

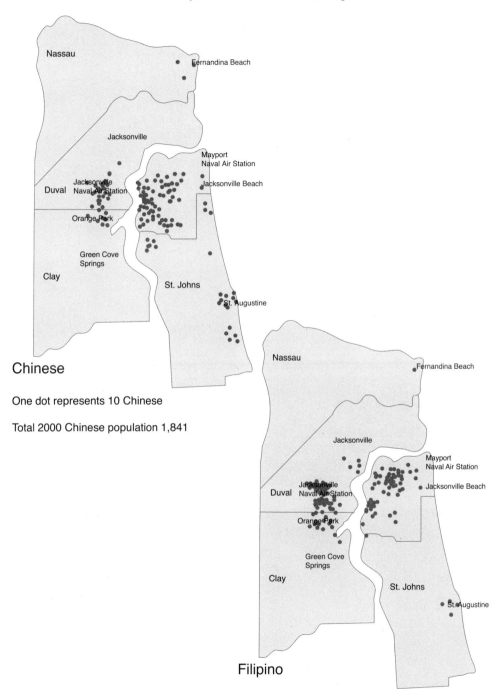

Chinese

One dot represents 10 Chinese

Total 2000 Chinese population 1,841

Filipino

One dot represents 100 Filipinos

Total 2000 Filipino population 12,178

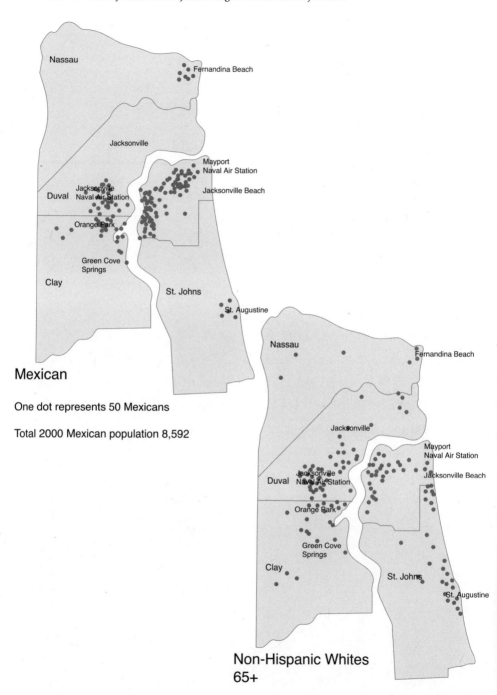

Mexican

One dot represents 50 Mexicans

Total 2000 Mexican population 8,592

Non-Hispanic Whites 65+

One dot represents 750 Non-Hispanic Whites 65+

Total 2000 Non-Hispanic White population 65+ 99,210

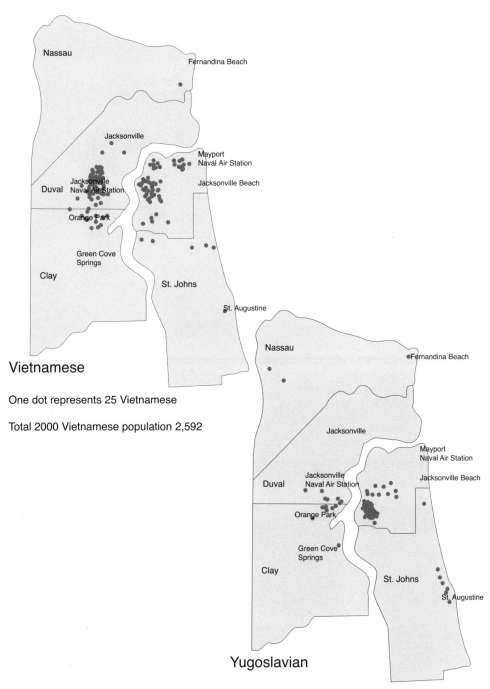

Vietnamese

One dot represents 25 Vietnamese

Total 2000 Vietnamese population 2,592

Yugoslavian

One dot represents 25 Yugoslavians
Total 2000 Yugoslavian population 3,864
Includes Croats, Macedonians, Serbians, and Slovenes

Conclusion

Florida's population has been diverse since the first humans arrived here an estimated 12,000 years ago. Though racially homogenous, the Indians developed distinct cultures in different parts of Florida largely based on what the environment could offer. With the Spanish, a new race arrived in Florida, one whose technologies were more advanced than those of the native population. The Spanish also brought with them slaves from Africa. Henceforth, Florida became the home of the world's three largest races.

Once it was annexed by the United States, Florida's racial, ancestral, and religious diversity began to increase. Whites of Anglo-Saxon heritage became dominant, and black slaves were brought in to provide labor. Like other southern states, Florida has a long history of racial violence. Between 1882 and 1930, the state had the highest ratio of lynchings per 100,000 blacks in the nation: 79.8 compared to Mississippi with 52.8 (the nation's second highest). Although physical violence between blacks and whites has greatly diminished, racial issues involving education and housing persist. Fortunately, throughout the state, private citizens, action groups, religious institutions, and various state and local government agencies remain vigilant in their efforts to protect the rights of the many and varied subgroups (including those from foreign nations) within its population.

Racially and culturally, Florida's identity remained distinctly "Southern" until well into the twentieth century. By 1950, however, increasing numbers of non-Hispanic white retirees, most from northern states, began to arrive, many claiming ancestries and religious affiliations previously little known or nonexistent in Florida. As a result, parts of the state began quite obviously to lose their Southern culture.

Following the success of the Cuban Revolution in 1959, hundreds of thousand of Cubans went into exile, most settling in South Florida. This migration precipitated an even larger migration from elsewhere in Latin America and from non-Hispanic islands in the Caribbean. Although the influx is much lighter from outside the Western Hemisphere, the state is now attracting thousands of people from Asia. Relatively few immigrants, however, are coming directly from Europe, and virtually none are arriving from Africa. In sum, however, the state is becoming, in terms of its races, ancestries, and religions, as complex as New York and California—a fact that this atlas hopefully has illuminated.

Some readers may have noticed that I do not use the term "melting pot" to describe the increasingly intense and complicated interactions among the state's races and ancestry groups. Despite examples of outstanding progress in the relations among various groups, it is still too early to declare Florida a melting pot. Barriers imposed by the dominant groups still impede the progress of certain minorities. In turn, some minorities, wishing to preserve their cultural heritage, erect barriers around themselves. In Florida, as elsewhere in the United States, debate between multiculturalists and assimilationists continues over the best strategies for resolving racial and ethnic conflict. The multiculturalists appeal for mutual respect among the nation's many distinct cultures, while the latter believe that greater efforts should be made to create one national culture. Through proper leadership, an accommodation may develop between the two opposing views. I hope that this atlas will contribute to a greater degree of harmony among the state's racial and ancestral groups as well as within and among its religious denominations.

References

Boswell, Thomas D., and James R. Curtis. 1983. *The Cuban-American Experience: Culture, Images, and Perspective*. Totowa, N.J.: Rowman & Allanheld.

Boswell, Thomas D., and Emily Skep. 1995. *Hispanic National Groups in Metropolitan Miami*. Miami, Fla.: Cuban American National Council.

Brooks, William E. 1965. *History Highlights of Florida Methodism*. Fort Lauderdale, Fla.: Tropical Press.

Bullock, James R. 1987. *Heritage and Hope: a Story of Presbyterians in Florida*. Orlando, Fla.: Synod of Florida, Presbyterian Church (U.S.A.).

Burns, Allan F. 1993. *Maya in Exile: Guatemalans in Florida*. Philadelphia: Temple University Press.

Castro, Max J., and Thomas D. Boswell. 2002. *The Dominican Diaspora Revisited: Dominicans and Dominican-Americans in a New Century*. Coral Gables, Fla.: Dante Fascell North-South Center.

Colburn, David R., and Jane L. Landers. 1995. *The African American Heritage of Florida*. Gainesville: University Press of Florida.

Corbitt, Duvon C. 1945. "The Last Spanish Census of Pensacola, 1820." *Florida Historical Quarterly* 24 (1): 30–38.

Cruz, Arturo J., and Jaime Suchliki. 1990. *The Impact of Nicaraguans in Miami*. Coral Gables, Fla.: Graduate School of International Studies, University of Miami.

Cushman, Joseph D. 1965. *A Goodly Heritage: The Episcopal Church in Florida, 1821–1892*. Gainesville: University of Florida Press.

Dunkle, John R. 1958. "Population Change as an Element in the Historical Geography of St. Augustine." *Florida Historical Quarterly* 37 (1): 3–32.

Dunn, Marvin. 1997. *Black Miami in the Twentieth Century*. Gainesville: University Press of Florida.

Foster, Charles C., and Veronica Huss. 1991. *Conchtown USA: Bahamian Fisherfolk in Riviera Beach, Florida*. Gainesville: University Presses of Florida.

Gannon, Michael. 1965. *Cross in the Sand: The Early Catholic Church in Florida, 1513–1870*. Gainesville: University of Florida Press.

Gaustad, Edwin Scott, and Philip L. Barlow. 2001. *New Historical Atlas of Religion in America*. New York: Oxford University Press.

Gordon, Jessica. 2005. "Religion in Transition." *Explores: Research at the University of Florida* 10 (spring): 38–42.

Green, Henry A., and Marcia K. Zerivitz. 1991. *Jewish Life in Florida: A Documentary Exhibit from 1793 to the Present*. Coral Gables, Fla.: MOSAIC, Inc.

Grenier, Guillermo J., and Alex Stepick III, eds. 1992. *Miami Now! Immigration, Ethnicity, and Social Change.* Gainesville: University Press of Florida.

Halvorson, Peter L., and William M. Newman. 1978. *Atlas of Religious Change in America, 1952–1971.* Washington: Glenmary Research Center.

Hill, Samuel S., ed. 1984. *Encyclopedia of Religion in the South.* Macon, Ga.: Mercer.

Joiner, Edward Earl. 1972. *A History of Florida Baptists.* Jacksonville, Fla.: Convention Press.

Jones, Dale E. et al. *Religious Congregations and Membership in the United States.* Atlanta: Glenmary Research Center. (Censuses for 1952, 1972, 1982, and 1992 published under the title *Churches and Church Membership in the United States*).

Jones, Maxine D. 1996. "The African-American Experience in Twentieth-Century Florida." In *The New History of Florida*, ed. Michael Gannon, 373–90. Gainesville: University Press of Florida.

Laing, Craig R. 2002. "The Latter-Day Saint Diaspora in the United States and the South." *Southeastern Geographer* 42 (2): 228–47.

Lamme, Ary J., and Christopher F. Meindl. 2002. "A Vibrant Cultural Boundary in Florida." *Southeastern Geographer* 42 (2): 274–95.

Lamme, Ary J., and Raymond Oldakowski. 1982. "Vernacular Areas in Florida." *Southeastern Geographer.* 42 (2): 99–109.

Landers, Jane. 1996. "Free and Slave." In *The New History of Florida*, ed. Michael Gannon, 167–82. Gainesville: University Press of Florida.

Lee, David. 1992. "Black Districts in Southeastern Florida." *Geographical Review* 82 (4): 375–87.

Martin, David. 1991. *Tongues of Fire: The Explosion of Protestantism in Latin America.* Cambridge, Mass.: Blackwell.

McAlister, L. N. 1959. "Pensacola during the Second Spanish Period." *Florida Historical Quarterly* 37 (3): 281–327.

McNally, Michael J. 1982. *Catholicism in South Florida, 1868–1968.* Gainesville: University Presses of Florida.

Milanich, Jerald T. 1995. *Florida Indians and the Invasion from Europe.* Gainesville: University Press of Florida.

Miller, Jake C. 1984. *The Plight of Haitian Refugees.* New York: Praeger.

Mohl, Raymond A. 1987. "Black Immigrants: Bahamians in Early Twentieth-Century Miami." *Florida Historical Quarterly* 65 (3): 271–97.

———. 1990. "Florida's Changing Demography: Population Growth, Urbanization, and Latinization." *Environmental and Urban Issues* 17 (Winter 1990): 22–30.

———. 1990. "Miami: New Immigrant City." In *Search for the Sunbelt: Historical Perspectives on a Region*, ed. Raymond A. Mohl, 149–75. Knoxville: University of Tennessee Press.

———. 1990. "On the Edge: Blacks and Hispanics in Metropolitan Miami since 1959." *Florida Historical Quarterly* 69 (1): 37–56.

———. 1996. "From Migration to Multiculturalism: A History of Florida Immigration."

In *The New History of Florida*, ed. Michael Gannon, 391–417. Gainesville: University Press of Florida.

Mormino, Gary R., and George E. Pozzetta. 1987. *The Immigrant World of Ybor City: Italians and Their Latin Neighbors in Tampa, 1885–1985*. Champaign-Urbana: University of Illinois Press.

Portes, Alejandro, and Alex Stepick. 1993. *City on the Edge: The Transformation of Miami*. Berkeley: University of California Press.

Pozzetta, George E. 1974. "Foreign Colonies in South Florida, 1865–1910." *Tequesta* 34:45–56.

———. 1974. "Foreigners in Florida: A Study of Immigration Promotion, 1865–1910." *Florida Historical Quarterly* 53 (2): 164–80.

———. 1989. "The Chinese Encounter with Florida, 1865–1920." *Chinese America: History and Perspectives* 2: 43–58.

Rieff, David. 2000. *Going to Miami: Exiles, Tourists and Refugees in the New America*. Gainesville: University of Press of Florida.

Rosenthal, Eric. 1975. "The Equivalence of United States Census Data for Persons of Russian Stock or Descent with American Jews." *Demography* 12 (2): 275–90.

Sheskin, Ira. 1996. *Jewish Demographic Study: Main Report*. Boca Raton, Fla.: Jewish Federation of South Palm Beach County.

Smith, Brian H. 1998. *Religious Politics in Latin America, Pentecostal vs. Catholic*. Notre Dame, Ind.: University of Notre Dame Press.

Stepick, Alex. 2003. *This Land Is Our Land: Immigrants and Power in Miami*. Berkeley: University of California Press.

Tebeau, Charlton W. 1971. *A History of Florida*. Coral Gables, Fla.: University of Miami Press.

U.S. Census Bureau. 1910. *Religious Bodies: 1906*. Washington, D.C.: U.S. Government Printing Office. Censuses also were taken in 1916, 1926, and 1936.

———. *United States Census 2000*. http://www.census.gov/main/www/cen2000.html.

Winsberg, Morton D. 1979. "Housing Segregation of a Predominantly Middle Class Population: Residential Patterns Developed by the Cuban Immigration into Miami, 1950–74." *American Journal of Economics and Sociology* 38 (4): 403–18.

———. 1983. "The Changing Distribution of the Black Population in Florida Cities, 1970–1980." *Urban Affairs Quarterly* 18 (3): 361–70.

———. 1983. "Ethnic Competition for Residential Space in Miami, 1970–80." *American Journal of Economics and Sociology* 42 (3): 304–14.

———. 1983. "Non-Hispanic White Elderly in Southern Florida, 1950–1980." *Geographical Review* 73 (4): 447–49.

———. 1989. "Suburbanization of Higher Income Blacks in Major Metropolitan Statistical Areas." *Urban Geography* 10 (4): 172–77.

———. 1993. "The Changing South: Regional Migratory Streams to Different Parts of Florida." *Southeastern Geographer* 33 (1): 110–21.

———. 1994. "Urban Population Redistribution under the Impact of Foreign Immigration and More Recently, Natural Disaster: The Case of Miami." *Urban Geography* 15 (5): 487–94.

———. 1999. "Racial Segregation of the Affluent and Poor in Nineteen Florida MSAs." *Florida Geographer* 30: 70–93.

Zelinsky, Wilbur. 1961. "An Approach to the Religious Geography of the United States: Patterns of Church Membership in 1952." *Annals of the Association of American Geographers* 51 (2): 139–93.

Morton D. Winsberg is emeritus professor of geography at Florida State University. He is one of the contributors to *The Atlas of Florida* (UPF: 1st edition, 1981; revised edition, 1996) and *Florida Weather* (UPF: 1st edition, 1990; revised edition, 2003).